# Brethren Brush with
# GREATNESS

32 stories by Frank Ramirez

illustrated by Kermon Thomasson

THE BRETHREN CELEBRATE 300 YEARS

*Brethren Brush with Greatness*
32 Stories by Frank Ramirez

Copyright © 2008 by Brethren Press®. Brethren Press is a trademark of the Church of the Brethren General Board, 1451 Dundee Avenue, Elgin, IL 60120.

Illustrator: Kermon Thomasson
Design: The Concept Mill

Library of Congress Cataloging-in-Publication Data

Ramirez, Frank, 1954-
  Brethren brush with greatness : 32 stories / by Frank Ramirez ; illustrated by Kermon Thomasson.
    p. cm.
  Summary: "A collection of thirty-two stories that focuses on individuals whose lives have touched the Church of the Brethren—famous people who were somehow related to the Brethren; Brethren who, themselves, became famous; and famous people who, legend has it, were members of the Church of the Brethren"—Provided by publisher.
  ISBN 978-0-87178-095-9
  1. Church of the Brethren—Biography. I. Title.

  BX7841.R35 2008
  286'.5—dc22
  [B]
                                    2008010469

12  11  10  09  08      1  2  3  4  5  6
Printed in the United States of America

*This book is one of several Brethren Press publications displaying the mark of the 300^th Anniversary of the Brethren (1708-2008). It represents the theme "Surrendered to God, Transformed by Christ, Empowered by the Spirit."*

# CONTENTS

**Introduction**

*To our son Francisco Daniels Ramirez with love.*
*It's just great that you're here.*

# INTRODUCTION

Perhaps the idea of a book called *Brethren Brush with Greatness* is a contradiction in terms. The Brethren don't define greatness in the same way as the world. The culture might be concerned with the glitzy, the glamorous, the rich, the powerful, but our definition of greatness is Aunt Mabel who bakes the best apple betty in the world. Or maybe it's old George who takes soup to folks who are sick. Or the quilting ladies who comfort folks at the local domestic violence shelter with comforters.

Sitting in our pews are aging "seagoing cowboys" and volunteers young and old who travel all over swinging hammers with their district disaster relief teams. There are prayer warriors who keep God on the line for hours without tiring and the folks who get the beef and broth just right for love feast. These are our heroes.

Not that we expect anyone else to know or care. In the Gospel of John we read, "He was in the world, and the world came into being through him; yet the world did not know him" (1:10). We're canny enough to accept that the world doesn't recognize our heroes.

With regard to the people we think of as famous, there are no layers of protection and fences to keep us from face-to-face interaction with them. Take the late Donald F. Durnbaugh. He was a scholar recognized the world over and honored by folks beyond our circles, but there wasn't a question we couldn't ask him. Don would listen patiently to every query that came his way and give a thoughtful and precise answer. And he'd tell a joke that would leave us laughing.

Come to think of it, it was that way with all the professors, moderators, executives, administrators, writers, and pastors I've ever met in our circles. I remember my first class at Bethany Theological Seminary. It was 1976 and I'd been told that we had a world-class faculty. I was in a New Testament class with Dr. Graydon F. Snyder. We were still getting used to the fact we were supposed to call him Grady, when in burst Dr. Robert Neff. Bob immediately began to berate Grady not about some theological point, but about the World Series—Yankees versus Reds. Then somehow the topic shifted to the question of who was going to win at racquetball later in the week!

Ph.D. M.D. We're just folks. If one of us were great in the eyes of the world, the rest of us might not be all that impressed. After all, our definition of greatness is Jesus. We are a Jesus church. Long before people invented WWJD bracelets, we would ask what would Jesus do, and then that's what we did.

Twenty-nine years ago, when I was a student at Bethany, my wife, Jennie, went into labor three months early and nearly bled to death. In hopes of saving Jennie's life, we were rushed through Friday night rush hour traffic to a downtown Chicago hospital specializing in neonatology, but our doctor did not expect that our baby would make it. In an era long before cell phones and text messaging, the word went out. Without anyone organizing anything, students and faculty gathered at the seminary chapel for a prayer vigil. Now that's greatness!

Jennie survived and so did Francisco Daniels Ramirez—with relatively few long-term problems, other than sharing his father's love for the music of Bob Dylan. A few days after Cisco was born, faculty members Don Miller and Nancy Faus donned sterile gowns and masks to perform anointing for healing for the three of us, and that too is a mark of our greatness that comes from following our Lord and Savior Jesus Christ.

So, despite having defined greatness one way, in these pages you will meet those people who are famous as the world defines fame. Some are Brethren and others have touched the lives of Brethren.

This book cannot be exhaustive. Some stories are interesting but for various reasons haven't been included. For example, you might not know that the sister of singer Patsy Cline attends a Brethren church; or that the famous author Studs Terkel was best friends with one of our own Brethren writers, Kermit Eby; or that Ed Asner narrated *Little, Middle, Tall*, the video version of the Brethren Press children's books.

Then there are those stories we've heard of but can't corroborate. The Brethren connection to Mae West is one that comes to mind. I heard that one from several people, but Person A referred me to Person B who said if I wanted to know anything I should talk to Person C who referred me to Person A! If you want more details then why don't you come up and see me sometime?

There are some that are just stories—we don't know anything else about them. And there are some, no doubt, who are known to you but unknown to any of us involved with this book. We hope that you will be prompted to tell your stories.

I received a lot of help as I wrote this book. First and foremost, I want to thank Ken Shaffer, the director of the

Brethren Historical Library and Archives at Elgin, Illinois. Ken is a celebrity in his own right, at least among those of us who love Brethren history. I also want to thank intern Logan Condon, who assisted Ken and me in researching this book.

Thank you, Nancy Klemm and Wendy McFadden, in Brethren Press, for your faith in me and your constant encouragement. Thanks to all who responded to my queries, including Brian Sell, Jane Henney, and especially Don Murray! Thanks also to Jeanine Wine and Francisco Ramirez for your help in finding resources. Thanks to the late Ken Morse, who provided personal encouragement while he was alive and a lot of inspiration and direction through his book *Preaching in a Tavern.* I want to thank all Brethren, past and present, who've gone along with this crazy idea that the Bible belongs to all of us, that none of us is all that special because there's only one Lord and we want to be like him. Thank you as well for welcoming me into this family of faith and accepting me as one of us.

Thanks most of all to my wife, Jennie Elizabeth Ramirez, long-suffering and patient, who did not get tired of my talking about this assignment.

God bless you all.

*Frank Ramirez*

# THE DUNKER WHO IMPRESSED BENJAMIN FRANKLIN

**BENJAMIN FRANKLIN • 1706-1790**

*Among the Founding Fathers, there's no question in my mind that Benjamin Franklin would have been the most fascinating—and fun—to know.*

Unlike most of the founding generation (with the exception of Alexander Hamilton), Franklin was born into poverty. He acquired wealth by hard work as a printer and went on to become a writer, diplomat, inventor, scientist, aphorist, abolitionist, founder of a nation, and general observer of the human condition. Though there had been many scientists before him, Franklin was one of the first to see science not as an academic pursuit, but as a means for improving the life of the ordinary person. His lightning rod was probably the first real instance of applied science. He also invented the Franklin stove, bi-focals, and many other practical devices. He developed the first public library and fire department. And he was quick-witted.

But if we are impressed by Benjamin Franklin, it is fascinating to note that he was impressed by one of us—or at least by someone he *thought* was one of us. In his *Autobiography* Franklin pays tribute to the Brethren in general, and to Michael Wohlfahrt (1687-1741) in particular, for our willingness to be open to new light. Wohlfahrt was a German immigrant who settled in the Colonies in the 1720s. To an outsider, Wohlfahrt might have been identified as one of the Dunkers, or Brethren, but he was, in reality, active in the breakaway body that was associated with the mystic separatist Conrad Beissel, who founded the Ephrata Cloister. One of the central elements of that Brethren experiment was the willingness to revisit the scriptures for new light.

While complaining about his political opponents, the Friends, or Quakers as they were known, Franklin says of the Dunkers (by the way, Franklin refers to Wohlfahrt as Welfare):

> Those embarrassments that the Quakers suffered from having established and published it as one of their principles that no kind of war was lawful and which, being once published they could not afterwards, however they might change their minds, easily get rid of, reminds me of, what I think, a more prudent conduct in another sect among us, that of the Dunkers.

I was acquainted with one of its founders, Michael Welfare. Soon after it appeared, he complained to me that they were grievously calumniated by the zealots of other persuasions, and charged with abominable principles and practices, to which they were utter strangers. I told him this had always been the case with new sects, and that, to put a stop to such abuse, I imagined it might be well to publish the articles of their belief, and the rules of their discipline. He said that it had been proposed among them, but not agreed to, for this reason: "When we were first drawn together as a society," said he, "it had pleased God to enlighten our minds so far as to see that some doctrines, which were once esteemed truths, were errors, and that others, which we had esteemed errors, were real truths. From time to time he has been pleased to afford us farther light, and our principles have been improving, and our errors diminishing. Now we are not sure that we arrived at the end of this progression and at the perfection of spiritual or theological knowledge, and we fear that if we should once print our confession of faith, we should feel ourselves as if bound and confined by it, and perhaps be unwilling to receive farther improvement, and our successors still more so, as conceiving what their elders and founders had done, to be something sacred—never to be departed from."

This modesty in a sect is perhaps a singular instance in the history of mankind. Every other sect, supposing itself in possession of all truth and that those who differ are so far in the wrong, like a man traveling in foggy weather, those at some distance before him on the road he sees wrapped up in the fog, as well as those behind him, and also the people in the fields on each side, but near him all appears clear, though in truth he is as much in the fog as any of them. (Brumbaugh 527-28)

Franklin refers again to Wohlfahrt in his newspaper, *The Pennsylvania Gazette,* in an account of his visit to Philadelphia on September 24, 1734, to denounce the sinfulness of its inhabitants:

Yesterday morning Michael Welfare, one of the Christian Philosophers of Conestoga, appeared . . . in the Habit of a Pilgrim, his Hat of Linnen, his Beard at full Length, and a long Staff in his Hand. He declared himself sent by Almighty God, to denounce Vengeance against the Iniquity and Wickedness of the Inhabitants of this City and Province, without speedy Repentance. The Earnestness of his Discourse, which continu'd near a quarter of an Hour; the Vehemence of his Action, and the Importance of what he delivered, commanded the Attention of a Multitude of People.

Before someone singles out Franklin as a champion of the Brethren, however, it's worth noting that Franklin resented German involvement in local politics, especially because they tended to support the Quakers. He was also suspicious of their love for their own language and retaining their ethnic identity. In his essay "The Support of the Poor," written to Peter Collinson on May 9, 1753, he says:

For I remember when they modestly declined intermeddling in our Elections, but now they come in droves, and carry all before them, except in one or two Counties; Few of their children in the Country learn English; they import many Books from Germany; and of the six printing houses in the Province, two are entirely German, two half German half English, and but two entirely English; They have one German News-paper, and one half German. Advertisements intended to be general are now printed in Dutch and English; the Signs in our Streets have inscriptions in both languages, and in some places only German.

It didn't help that as a printer Franklin found himself in direct competition with the Christopher Sauer Press. The original Christopher Sauer, a German immigrant, was himself not Brethren but was certainly sympathetic to them. His groundbreaking press produced the first Bible in a European language in the New World. He published newspapers, periodicals, books, and religious materials in both German and English. An immigrant who arrived with nothing but wonder at the opportunities available in the Colonies, he went on to practice many trades successfully. He was in his own right a polymath like Franklin. Perhaps it was inevitable that they should become competitors.

In his book *The Christopher Sauers*, Brethren historian Stephen L. Longenecker chronicles the competition between the rival printers. On more than one occasion, Franklin attempted to eliminate the Sauers as competitors by controlling credit and supplies, such as rags that were used in the production of paper along with the supply of ink. This forced the German printers to manufacture their own supplies. However, Franklin's attempts to corner the German-speaking market failed.

The elder Sauer's son, Christopher Sauer II, continued the printing business and was himself baptized Brethren. The competition continued as Franklin attempted to produce a German-language paper. There are instances in which they seem to have cooperated, but at other times the competition was not so friendly.

It seems certain that the admiration Franklin had for the Brethren was limited to those who were not in direct competition with him. Although in many ways he transcended his era, he also believed and perpetuated prejudices against those whom he perceived as different from himself.

# THE BRETHREN WHO FED GEORGE WASHINGTON

## GEORGE WASHINGTON • 1732-1799

2

*GEORGE WASHINGTON SLEPT HERE! Now that's a familiar sign— especially in the East.*

The first president of the United States is still visible everywhere—on the dollar bill, on the quarter, in ads and parodies, and on posters. And rightly so. Washington was a towering figure—and as human as the rest of us. It was hard enough for his successors to fill his shoes. It was even harder for the first president to fit into his own clothes. It's said that during his early planter days he ordered his clothes from Great Britain in exchange for the tobacco he shipped overseas and that he tended to give the wrong sizes, perhaps out of vanity.

Well, how about GEORGE WASHINGTON ATE HERE? If eating was involved, you can be pretty sure there were Brethren near at hand. And so it was in this case.

Washington's wide experience made him perhaps the one leader who was able to cement a loose confederacy of cantankerous small nations together in a battle for independence and then later lead them in a battle for dependence upon each other. The Brethren were lukewarm at best about the revolution led by General George Washington. They were grateful for the religious freedom granted them in the British Colonies, especially Pennsylvania. And they believed it was their duty, as long it did not conflict with their first allegiance to their Lord Jesus, to respect and submit to the present government.

Moreover, because the Brethren were opposed to participation in war, they were not ready to take up arms in the struggle for independence. Nevertheless, this nonresistant stance meant they were also more likely to pay their taxes or allow the tax collectors to take what they pleased from their properties, in sharp contrast to the attitude of many so-called patriots who had no intention of supporting the Army or the Continental Congress no matter what their needs.

After the matter was settled, however, Brethren were ready to support and respect the new government. And so it is not in the least surprising to hear that one family, at least, felt honored to host the great man.

This story comes to us from James Quinter, Brethren teacher, preacher, and publisher, in the May 28, 1878, issue of *The Primitive Christian and the Pilgrim*. Quinter had traveled to Virginia in order to officiate at a funeral and lead a week's worth of services. One of the people he visited was Jacob Forrer, who told Quinter the following story about his mother and her memory of having dinner with George Washington. Ms. Ebersole (Quinter never mentions her first name) was just a girl when Washington came calling in the Hagerstown, Maryland, area to find a site for the new nation's capital.

Having lived to the age she had, she was acquainted with the early history of our country, and took delight in relating events that had happened under her notice. She remembered very distinctly General Washington and his appearance. She related to her children a visit that he made to her father's family while she was at home. When he and a number of the men of note, of his time, were selecting a site for the [capital] of the United States, they visited the country about Hagerstown, as that place was thought of as the site of the seat of Government. The person in the company whose business it was to provide for the entertainment of the company, called at the house of Mr. Ebersole and desired to make preparations there for Gen. Washington and his suite to dine. Mr. Ebersole modestly suggested some other place, that of a more distinguished man than he felt himself to be, and one that he thought more worthy of the distinguished guest that was desiring entertainment than he himself was. But Gen. Washington had heard something of Mr. Ebersole, and desired to make his house his stopping-place. The use of the house was then granted to the company.

The General's company had its cooks and many of the conveniences needed for the preparation of the dinner. There were some things, however, they desired the family to furnish, and these were at once supplied. Sister Forrer [Ms. Ebersole] remembered the manner in which the company partook of the dinner, or the way in which they conducted themselves at the table. When they were seated, some thirty or more in number, Gen. Washington said grace, and there was no levity at the table, and no more talking than what the occasion called for. After dinner the General conversed awhile pleasantly with Mr. Ebersole, upon such subjects as he thought would be most agreeable to his host.

When the company was about leaving, the proper person asked for the bill; but he was told that the honor of entertaining such a company was a sufficient compensation. He, however, took out a ten dollar gold piece, and when it was refused, it was thrown down with the remark, "give it to the girls." (330)

Several questions remain. Quinter doesn't say when this all happened. It's not even clear from this account if the nation was still under the Articles of Confederation or if Washington had yet been elected president under the new Constitution, which happened in 1789. And who exactly scooped up the gold coin, a considerable sum in those days? Certainly the dinner itself was provided by Washington, who traveled with his own cooks.

These questions led to a little Internet research. Taking into account that in Washington's time Hagerstown was known as Elizabethtown, there is record of a visit by the president to that town in a letter dated October 20, 1790, from Washington "To the Inhabitants of Elizabeth Town and its vicinity." He mentions their "cordial welcome" with his "grateful and sincere acknowledgments." The letter, available in a handwritten version in the Washington Archives and reprinted in the November 3, 1790, edition of the *Gazette of the United States* (printed in Philadelphia), closes with a wish for their "temporal happiness and future felicity."

A letter written October 25, 1790, to William Temple Franklin, Esquire (grandson of Benjamin Franklin) of Philadelphia, apologizes for a delay in replying to an earlier letter because of "an excursion" on the Potomac, which probably included the Hagerstown stop.

Did the visit to the Ebersoles really happen? The exact details are probably impossible to determine. The present account is a retelling from memory by James Quinter of a visit with Jacob Forrer who remembered an accounting of the event remembered by his mother who was remembering the actual event many years before.

One thing, no, two things seem clear. The first is that the family remembered they'd been visited by George Washington. That's the sort of singular event that sticks in family lore and is probably based on truth.

The second is that if General Washington actually used his own cooks, he missed out on a genuine Brethren meal served up by an honest-to-goodness Brethren sister. Too bad. Or maybe it's just as well. Had Washington become addicted to Brethren cooking, he might have found it even more difficult to fit into his clothes!

# DANIEL BOONE—A "LEGEND" OF THE BRETHREN?

## 3

**DANIEL BOONE • 1734-1820**

*Of the great names*
*    which in our faces stare,*
*The General Boone,*
*    back-woodsman of Kentucky,*
*Was happiest amongst mortals any where;*
*For killing nothing but a bear or buck, he*
*Enjoyed the lonely vigorous, harmless days*
*Of his old age in wilds of deepest maze.*

So wrote Lord Byron in his epic poem *Don Juan*
(1822) about the man known as Daniel Boone.
By that time Boone had been dead barely two

years, but his legend had already begun to eclipse the extraordinary story of his life as a frontiersman who opened up the wild country of Kentucky to European settlers. Boone's exploits among the Indians as both sympathizer and adversary, his purported part in the Revolution (largely unproved—he seems not to have been a warrior), and his undoubted bravery were all the stuff of legend. Largely fictional biographies have made him famous on both the North American and European continents.

As a child it was easy to confuse the television portrayals of Daniel Boone and Davy Crockett who were both played by Fess Parker. The lyrics for the television series of the sixties, written by Vera Matson, did not have to be true to be exciting.

> *Daniel Boone was a man,*
> *Yes, a big man!*
> *He was brave, he was fearless*
> *And as tough as a mighty oak tree!*
> *From the coonskin cap on the top of ol' Dan*
> *To the heel of his rawhide shoe;*
> *The rippin'est, roarin'est, fightin'est man*
> *The frontier ever knew. . . .*

Though Boone didn't wear a coonskin hat or rawhide shoes, Fess Parker did, and that was good enough.

Brethren developed legends of their own about the frontiersman; that he was raised and baptized Brethren was one of them. Though the actual relationship is unclear, it's likely that there was a connection between the Boone family and the Brethren.

The Englishman Squire Boone, who emigrated to America in 1717, and his wife, Sarah, were known to be Quakers in Berks County, Pennsylvania, but there is evidence that they were disciplined by their church because at least two of their children—their oldest daughter, Sarah, and oldest son, Israel—married Brethren and presumably attended a German Baptist church.

Squire Boone moved his family through the Shenandoah Valley south to North Carolina by 1753 to an area settled by Brethren. During troubles with the Indians, the family temporarily abandoned their home to return to Virginia in 1759, but returned a few years later.

Three sons, Daniel, George, and young Squire, seem to have had some sort of association with the Brethren, especially Squire, who was for many years a Baptist minister, but may have served as a Brethren minister as well. Daniel and Squire were involved in land speculation in Kentucky and Missouri, and Brethren families were among those who purchased property from the brothers: the Leathermans, Hostetters, Shocks, Wises, Youngs, Bowers, Lastlys, Garrows, Taylors, and Rubles.

Daniel Boone is an appealing candidate for inclusion among the Brethren. Despite later stories about his participation in the Revolution, he served only as a noncombatant in the French and Indian War, hauling supply wagons for Washington. His relationships with the Indians were often harrowing, yet he showed great respect for their culture and in turn was respected by many of them.

But Daniel Boone, though a Christian believer, did not openly associate himself with any denomination. In 1816, in a letter to his sister-in-law Sarah Boone (brother Samuel's wife), he wrote,

> For my part I am as ignerent as a child. All the relegan I have is to Love and Fear God, beleve in Jesus Christ, dow all the good to my neighbors and myself that I can and dow as little harm as I can help and trust on God's mercy for the rest, and I believe God never made man[y] of my principal to be lost and I flatter myself, Dear Sister, that you are well on your way in Christianity. [All spelling original] (Flory 153)

Historians note that many of the Boone family descendants have been found on Brethren church rolls. Rolland F. Flory, in his book *Lest We Forget and Tales of Yester-Years, Volume III,* notes that in 1776 two Boones, Jacob and John, were fined for refusing to bear arms during the Revolutionary War. Many years later a Clara Boone was one of the first students at Manchester College in Indiana, while Amos Robert Boone and George N. Boone were remembered as graduates of McPherson College in Kansas.

But direct connections with the great pioneer himself are tenuous. If Daniel Boone was Brethren it remains unproven, and if this is a Brethren brush with greatness, it is only that—a brush!

# "A NOT-UNFEARED, HALF-WELCOME GUEST"

## HARRIET LIVERMORE • 1788-1868

## 4

*John Greenleaf Whittier (1807-1892) was known as the Quaker Poet. He was an abolitionist and was once forced to flee through a hail of bullets from an unfriendly audience.* He was active in literature, politics, and life. Known for his 759-line-poem, *Snow-Bound: A Winter Idyll*, published in 1866, Whittier provides striking images of his childhood home in the Merrimack Valley of Massachusetts, along with descriptions of the members of the household, including their "not-unfeared, half-welcome guest," to whom eighty lines are devoted. Hardly flattering, the excerpts given here describe a woman who was a frequent visitor in the Whittier home and had a significant effect on the Brethren as well:

*Another guest that winter night*
*Flashed back from lustrous eyes the light. . . .*
*She sat among us, at the test,*
*A not unfeared, half-welcome guest,*
*Rebuking with her cultured phrase*
*Our homeliness of words and ways.*
*A certain pard-like, treacherous grace*
*Swayed the lithe limbs and dropped the lash,*
*Lent the white teeth their dazzling flash;*
*And under low brows, black with night,*
*Rayed out at times a dangerous light;*
*The sharp heat-lightnings of her face*
*Presaging ill to him whom Fate*
*Condemned to share her love or hate.*
*A woman tropical, intense*
*In thought and act, in soul and sense,*

*She blended in a like degree*
*The vixen and the devotee,*
*Revealing with each freak of feint*
*The temper of Petruchio's Kate,*
*The raptures of Siena's saint.*
*Her tapering hand and rounded wrist*
*Had facile power to form a fist;*
*The warm, dark languish of her eyes*
*Was never safe from wrath's surprise.*
*Brows saintly calm and lips devout*
*Knew every change of scowl and pout;*
*And the sweet voice had notes more high*
*And shrill for social battle-cry.*
*Since then what old cathedral town*
*Has missed her pilgrim staff and gown,*
*What convent-gate has held its lock*

*Against the challenge of her knock!*
*. . . Where'er her troubled path may be,*
*The Lord's sweet pity with her go!*
*The outward wayward life we see,*
*The hidden springs we may not know.*
*Nor is it given us to discern*
*What threads the fatal sisters spun,*
*Through what ancestral years has run*
*The sorrow with the woman born,*

*What forged her cruel chain of moods,*
*What set her feet in solitudes,*
*And held the love within her mute,*
*What mingled madness in the blood*
*A life-long discord and annoy,*
*Water of tears with oil of joy,*
*And hid within the folded bud*
*Perversities of flower and fruit.*

The woman Whittier describes as the "pilgrim stranger" was Harriet Livermore who, when she read Whittier's description of her, flung the book across the room.

It has been said by some that if all had gone according to plan, Harriet Livermore would have been a wealthy socialite. She was born into a prominent New England family, but when her fiancé spurned her (both families disapproved of the marriage), she abandoned society, cut her long hair, gave away her finery, adopted a severe garb, and became one of the best-known preachers of her era.

Televangelists aside, the ministry is not a profession that promises great wealth. Harriet lived in poverty most of her life, but she rose to a prominence shared by few women of her time. She preached four times in the U.S. Congress before four different presidents, perhaps in part because her father, grandfather, and uncle served in Congress. That grandfather was one of the framers of the Bill of Rights. She traveled across the United States, Europe, and the Holy Land, often living from hand to mouth. Her message focused on the imminent apocalypse, and she preached wherever she was granted an audience.

And that included the Brethren. She may have been a "half-welcome guest" in Whittier's house, but she was welcomed in many Dunker congregations, including the Philadelphia church, where she was invited to preach by Brethren minister Peter Keyser, Jr., in August of 1826. Like the Brethren, she spoke without manuscript or notes. She often said that preaching from a manuscript was only reading. As the result of Harriet's preaching that day, one of her converts was the eighteen-year-old Sarah Righter, who was baptized and went on to become a famous preacher herself, the second woman (after Catharine Hummer) to preach among the Brethren. Though raised in the church, Sarah was not yet baptized and still wore fashionable clothing rather than the plain garb of the Brethren. Years later Sarah's son would speak of that day: "Here it was that my mother heard The Pilgrim Stranger and as the first fruits of her labors in Philadelphia was the conversion of my mother whom Harriet Livermore ever afterwards called 'my daughter,' as Paul called Timothy his son, and was not lacking in parental solicitude for her welfare" (Livermore 95). Harriet would later write of that day, "In all of my visits never have I given and received greater satisfaction" (Livermore 73).

Sarah Righter Major (she later married and took her husband's last name) became the lightning rod for a great deal of controversy. However, an Annual Meeting delegation sent to silence her refused to do so after hearing her preach, for she had demonstrated she could out-preach them all.

Brethren book collector, historian, and antiquarian Abraham Harley Cassel was an admirer of both Harriet Livermore and Sarah Righter Major. He himself heard Sarah preach when he was only eighteen and the effect was lasting. Cassel collected the papers and writings of Harriet Livermore and assisted S. T. Livermore who wrote the first biography of that woman, titled *Harriet Livermore: The "Pilgrim Stranger"* (1884), after the famous poem. Cassel once wrote in her defense that "She had all the faults that Whittier speaks of, but while he appears to have been so well acquainted with her, he must certainly have known her virtues as well as her faults" (Livermore 86).

Whittier himself tempered some of his criticism of Harriet by adding a preface to later editions of his poem in which he describes her as "a young woman of fine natural ability, enthusiastic, eccentric . . . equally ready to exhort in schoolhouse prayer meetings and dance in the Washington ballroom, while her father was a member of Congress."

Harriet's preaching, by all accounts, was extraordinarily powerful, but like all who challenge the way the rich or comfortable live, she had her detractors. Brethren historian Martin Grove Brumbaugh wrote about her passing in his 1899 history.

> Her last days were spent in the Almshouse in Philadelphia (Blockley), and at her death she was about to be consigned to a pauper's grave, when Sister Margaret F. Worrell appeared at the "Dead Room" and like one of old "begged the body" of the Pilgrim Stranger, took it to her own comfortable home in Germantown and gave it decent burial in the Germantown Cemetery of the Brethren.
>
> Here then sleeps the body of Harriet Livermore, "who had abhorred evil more, loved righteousness more, journeyed more amid perils, suffered more, preached and prayed more, wrote more, and wept more for Jesus than any other woman of whom we have a record" (Livermore 210). (189)

# THE WAGONS THAT WENT TO WAR WITHOUT A BRETHREN BROTHER

**5**

**JOHN CLEMENT STUDEBAKER AND FAMILY • 1799-1877**

*Studebaker wagons were known for their reliability, solid construction, and the company motto "Always give a little bit more than you promise."* Over three quarters of a million wagons rolled off the line, giving satisfaction to their owners as they carted across the continent—and that was *before* the Studebaker family thought to add a motor and a steering wheel.

The Studebakers were a pioneering Brethren family. Peter Studebaker emigrated from Germany in 1736. His grandson, Abraham Studabaker, Jr. (Studabaker, Studebaker, and Studybaker are all known spellings), moved to Darke County, Ohio, in 1808. Life on the frontier was harsh and difficult. When supplies such as flour and meal were needed, the twenty-eight-mile round trip to get provisions took two days.

Other Studebakers followed to Ohio. John Clement Studebaker built himself a wagon and moved to the state in 1835. Sixteen years later he moved the family farther west to South Bend, Indiana, and set up a blacksmith shop, where he posted his motto: "Owe no man anything but to love one another."

His five sons, Henry, Clement, John Mohler, Peter, and Jacob, soon set up a wagon-making business, copying the one their father had built. John Mohler invested $8,000 in the family business, all money he had earned in the West during the California Gold Rush. Although he never found gold, he struck it rich making wheelbarrows for the miners.

Eventually the Studebaker Company would become one of the world's first and premier automobile manufacturers, but not without facing a religious crisis within the family. During the Utah War of 1857-1858, the United States bought Studebaker wagons for military use against the Mormons. These were the same wagons the brothers had sold to the Mormons before they traveled west. Because of his Brethren convictions, Henry Studebaker allowed himself to be bought out of the firm. As one historian put it, "A good Dunkard could not help to arm one side, much less both." Brethren elders later visited and admonished the family because they sold their wagons to the military. Though the company continued to supply wagons to the army during the Civil War, the elder John Clement Studebaker prevented his son Jacob from serving in that war.

In 1868 the men called themselves the Studebaker Brothers Manufacturing Company, and by 1874 their sales had topped the million-dollar mark. Their wagons were essential equipment for the great westward migration. Manufacturing products known for their high quality, they also achieved worldwide fame. In 1880 the sultan of Zanzibar purchased two of their wagons after the Studebakers were honored at the Paris International Exposition of 1878.

With railways moving freight in the East, the brothers set up a branch office in St. Joseph, Missouri, to meet the needs of the farmers and other individuals. Peter Studebaker was in charge of manufacturing, and Clement Studebaker was in charge of sales. The contracts they drew up with each other read as follows: "I, Peter Studebaker, agree to sell all the wagons my brother Clem can make. (Signed) Peter Studebaker." And "I agree to make all he can sell. (Signed) Clem Studebaker."

In the twentieth century, the company successfully made the jump to horseless carriages, and the business became more successful than ever. The manufacturing part of the business continued until 1966. Celebrities such as Thomas Edison, Al Jolson, Jack Dempsey, Joe Louis, Judy Garland, Eleanor Roosevelt, and Ed Sullivan owned Studebakers. Even Brother Levi Bowman (1875-1977), an elderly, once-staid pastor at Jones Chapel in Virginia, is remembered by Kermon Thomasson as "tooling around the community in a vintage car called an Overland. Then he further jumped the traces by upping and buying one of the first Studebakers that came out with that Flash Gordon spaceship grill. It occasioned much mirth among the church members to see . . . Brother Levi so far ahead of his times . . . and the rest of us."

The Studebakers were not the only ones with a Brethren background to manufacture autos. Henry Clayton Stutz, a member of the Brethren congregation at Donnels Creek, not far from Dayton, Ohio, invented an efficient gasoline engine and by 1902 was successfully selling his automobiles. One of his cars won the first Indianapolis endurance race in 1911, and his Stutz Bearcat, which debuted in 1912, was known as the "most popular car of that day."

Certainly their Brethren background helped define their businesses. It was said of John Mohler Studebaker, who continued to work with the business until shortly before his death in 1917, that "the old Dunkard frugality never entirely disappeared" and that he kept a picture of his Brethren father on his desk in South Bend.

But Don Durnbaugh wryly notes in his history *Fruit of the Vine*:

> The Studebaker brothers and Stutz (and their biographers) credited their success in great part to the sturdy values of hard work, honesty, and integrity implanted by their early home and church training. It must also be reported, on the other hand, that as their ingenuity and hard work brought them high social status and wealth, they tended to transfer their denominational allegiances to more fashionable churches, except for Henry Studebaker who resigned from the family firm. The strict ethic of the conservative Dunkers had instilled useful moral traits, but the church discipline of the time demanded what increasingly seemed to be untenable constraints. (341)

# ABE LINCOLN'S "SECRET" BAPTISM

## ABRAHAM LINCOLN • 1809-1865

**6**

*It's a bit like the story some of us have heard here and there.* There was a fellow who knew a minister named H. Austin Cooper, who was pastor of Pleasant View Church of the Brethren in Burkittsville, Maryland. Cooper had written several books about the Pleasant View congregation and on several occasions told the story "about walking down the street in Frederick, Maryland, and seeing a box of old books out for the garbage man. He asked if he could have them and was given permission. It turned out that one of the books contained records of an older Brethren elder (I do not know the name). As he looked through the record, he saw a notation that 'On this date . . . in the 1850s . . . or '60s, I baptized  A L  At Point of Rocks' [a community in Frederick County]. Austin . . . felt certain that it was Abraham Lincoln because the records show that Abe was in the area on that date."

The stories of Lincoln's affiliation with the Brethren are known well enough among the Brethren to have been included as a sidebar written by Ken Morse in *The Brethren Encyclopedia* (743) and reprinted in his book *Preaching in a Tavern*. Morse wrote:

Although there is no documentary evidence that Abraham Lincoln was ever a member of any church, he has been claimed by many religious groups—including the Brethren. Presbyterians note that he attended Presbyterian churches, of which his wife was a member, in Springfield and Washington. Some of Lincoln's ancestors were Quakers. As a boy he attended a Baptist church. There are claims that he was a Swedenborgian, a spiritualist, a believer in universal salvation. A minister of the Christian Church was reported to have baptized Lincoln secretly in a creek near Springfield shortly before his inauguration as president of the United States.

This story is similar to one circulated by some Brethren who declared that Isaac Billheimer of Rossville or Heath, Indiana, either baptized Lincoln or was acquainted with the minister who did. This version claims that Lincoln met the minister one night near Springfield and that, after the baptism in a river, the minister returned home by train, the president promising that he would conform to the order of the church after completing his term of office. Another version of the Brethren baptism identifies a time of crisis in Lincoln's life in 1862 when, following a breakdown, he was said to have asked D. P. Sayler to baptize him in the Potomac River. Yet another anecdote tells of Lincoln's baptism by Elder George Wolfe.

Was Lincoln a secret Christian? *Lincoln's Unknown Private Life* (published in 1995) purports to be the memories of the African-American domestic Mariah Vance, who worked for the Lincolns in Springfield from 1850 to 1860. Forty years later, teenager Adah Sutton systematically wrote down Vance's memories, which included the revelation that Lincoln was baptized secretly by a Baptist minister in 1860, shortly before he took office. The manuscript, published only recently, may be one of the sources of the legend, though the veracity of the book has been questioned.

On the one hand, Lincoln was known to be a very religious person whose knowledge of the Bible was profound, and who could quote God's Word at will. On the other hand, he could also quote great slabs from Shakespeare's works as well, and some scholars have stated that his cadences are drawn more from Shakespeare than King James. It's also interesting to note that while Lincoln became a figure of legend, a much beloved leader whose death was mourned by the entire nation as ministers across the country extolled him as an example of Christian virtue, he had been an object of ridicule during his life and many in his own cabinet despised him.

In addition to the above observations, there are a couple of other reasons to question the reliability of the stories about Lincoln's Brethren baptism. The primary stumbling block is the element of secrecy. Brethren were against secret societies and associations and considered baptism to be a public act. Also Brethren expected that a person baptized into the Brethren faith would conform to gospel order, and that ought to include the matter of dress as well as the Brethren objection to war. Though the Civil War deeply pained Lincoln, he did not seem to doubt that war was necessary.

Jim Martin, in a lengthy *Restoration Quarterly* article titled "The Secret Baptism of Abraham Lincoln," examines many facets of the story that Lincoln was secretly baptized, in this case by a member of the Disciples of Christ. Martin concludes, as do most experts, that the story was the nineteenth-century equivalent of an urban legend. And that is probably where the matter is best left.

# THE SCULPTOR WHO FASHIONED THE DOORS OF CONGRESS

## WILLIAM H. RINEHART • 1825-1874

7

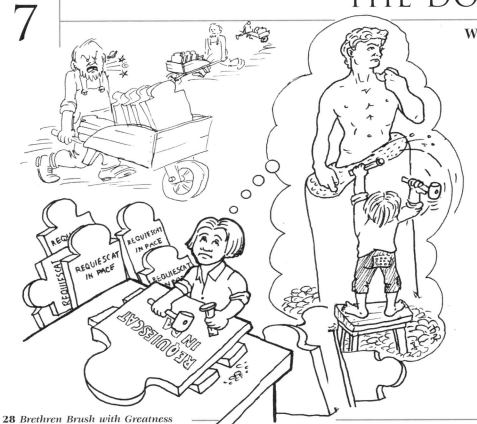

*On the East Portico of both the U.S. Senate and the House of Representatives are pairs of bronze doors sculpted by William H. Rinehart, one of the premier sculptors of his day.* The scenes, depicted from American history, are equally divided between stories of war and of peace.

The doors were finished in 1864 and 1867, respectively. There were few markets for Rinehart's work in the U.S., however, and more work than he could handle in Europe, so he returned to Europe and remained there for the rest of his short life.

One of Rinehart's most endearing and famous works is a sculpture of his mother that he completed after her death. It features Mary Snader Rinehart in her Dunker bonnet.

Mary proved her Brethren heritage when she insisted that her fiancé, Israel Rinehart, free his slaves before she would accept his marriage proposal. Israel's father had moved from the German Palatinate in 1733 and settled on a three-thousand-acre farm near Union Bridge, Maryland, in what is now Carroll County. That is where William Rinehart, the fifth of eight sons, was born and raised. It was said that William was more like his mother, a woman of gentle nature, than his father, who was a successful farmer and respected by his neighbors for his honesty and good management, but a stern disciplinarian.

William was known for his high spirits, and his companions remembered him for his capers and the Indian war dances he invented for their amusement. He had no great love for his studies, though his grades were passable, more, it was said, out of fear of his father than any enthusiasm for his schoolwork.

Once it became apparent that William was no great student, his father brought him home to work full time on the farm, but here too William proved to be less than successful. Next his father sent him to work with a stonemason, but the job proved too taxing physically, so William returned to the farm where he discovered his true talent.

Israel Rinehart had a marble quarry on his property, so he set his son to polishing tombstones and chiseling names and dates. William finally found something he was good at. By the time he was twenty-one, in the year 1846, he moved to the big city of Baltimore where he was apprenticed to one of the large stone-cutting companies. Over the next two years he mastered his craft, taking night classes in art to increase his competency. Soon he was winning awards and gaining attention. In 1855, with the help of art dealer William T. Walters, he left for Florence, Italy, where he lived most of the rest of his life. Though he returned briefly to Baltimore, he discovered that the United States could not provide the opportunities for an artist of his stature.

Rinehart was overwhelmed with commissions. Some were merely busts and sculptures for the well-to-do of America and Europe, but he also completed some extraordinary works inspired by classic themes of myth and legend—these in addition to completing the bronze doors for the U.S. Capitol, a project begun by the sculptor Thomas Crawford, who left the project unfinished at his death.

Rinehart's work included more than a hundred busts and thirty statues, as well as many bas-reliefs. His career was cut short, however, when, snowed under with many commissions, he unwisely decided to remain in Rome during the summer of 1874, rather than traveling to Switzerland as was his custom. Disease ran rampant in the ancient city during the hot months of the year, and Rinehart contracted tuberculosis, which claimed his life on October 28, 1874. He was only forty-nine years old.

Rinehart left the greater part of his estate for the benefit of art and artists. His executors invested well, and by 1891 the fund held more than one hundred thousand dollars. That sum was given to the Peabody Institute in Baltimore, where the Rinehart School of Sculpture was established as part of the Maryland Institute.

It is unlikely that the Brethren-born William Rinehart was ever baptized Brethren, nor does he seem to have practiced the faith.

The One About ────────────────────

# THE DUNKER WHO STOPPED
# THE RUNAWAY HORSE

### JOHN T. LEWIS • 1835-1906

## 8

*It's like a scene out of a movie. A buggy careening out of control down a steep hill, a young mother on board with her six-year-old daughter, the horse foaming from the mouth.* Together they speed toward a yawning abyss as other family members watch helplessly in horror, knowing there is nothing they can do to stop them.

Meanwhile, coming up the road from the other direction, our hero, riding a white charger and wearing a white hat, immediately recognizes the situation and speeds forward until he leaps through the air at exactly the right moment and . . .

No, it wasn't a scene from a movie and our hero wasn't wearing a white hat or riding a white horse. He was wearing his work clothes and sitting on the buckboard of his manure wagon. The only thing white about him was his long Dunker beard. This Dunker was known in that area of upper New York State as the only member of the Brethren in the area; he was anything but typical for the time.

John Lewis was born in Carroll County, Maryland, on January 10, 1835. He was baptized in the Pipe Creek congregation in 1853, at the age of eighteen. However, whether for economic or political reasons, he soon headed north around 1860, stopping first near Gettysburg, where he was living when the great battle took place in 1863.

Later he traveled on, making various stops in Pennsylvania, until in 1864 he reached Elmira, New York. There he worked at various jobs as a coachman, in a meat market, as a blacksmith, and for a time in the shop of A. Blivin and Sons. Eventually he settled in as a tenant farmer for Samuel L. Clemens' in-laws, the Langdon family near Quarry Hill. He married Mary A. Stover on July 27, 1865.

Lewis was a hard worker but found it difficult to make a living as a farmer. Mark Twain (as Samuel Clemens was better known) once wrote, "Lewis has worked mighty hard and remained mighty poor. At the end of each whole year's toil he can't show a gain of fifty dollars." According to some accounts, he was in debt by as much as nine hundred dollars to the Langdons, a huge sum by the standards of the day. Commenting on the debt, Twain said, ". . . he being conscientious & honest—imagine what it was to him to have to carry this stubborn hopeless load year in & year out."

But circumstances changed dramatically for John Lewis. The year was 1877. On August 23 Mark Twain's sister-in-law, Ida Langdon, along with her six-year-old daughter, Julia, and Nora, the nurse, were riding their carriage away from their home at Quarry Farm near Elmira, New York. Twain would remember the event in a letter to friends:

Well, sunset came & Ida the young & comely, . . . her little Julia & the nurse Nora drove out at the gate behind the new gray horse & started down the long hill—the high carriage receiving its load under the porte-cochere. Ida was seen to turn her face towards us across the fence & intervening lawn. Theodore waved good-by to her, for he did not know that her sign was a speechless appeal for help.

The next moment Livy said, "Ida's driving too fast down hill!" She followed it with a short scream "Her horse is running away!"

We could see two hundred yards down the descent. The buggy seemed to fly. It would strike obstructions & apparently spring the height of a man from the ground. Theodore & I left the shrieking crowd behind & ran down the hill bareheaded & shouting. A neighbor appeared at his gate—a tenth of a second too late! The buggy vanished past him like a thought. My last glimpse showed it for one instant, far down the descent, springing high in the air, out of a cloud of dust, & then it disappeared. As I flew down the road, my impulse was to shut my eyes & so delay for a moment the ghastly spectacle of mutilation & death I was expecting. (Wisbey, *Mark Twain in Elmira* 63-64).

From his vantage point as he traveled up the road, John Lewis could see immediately what was happening. He maneuvered his wagon so that it formed a V with a fence, forcing the out-of-control horse to run between the wagon and the fence. Lewis dismounted and waited. Only ten feet behind him was an abrupt turn in the road in front of an abyss through which buggy, passengers, and horse would surely plunge.

Lewis timed his jump, leapt through the air, and (once again in the words of Mark Twain) "gathered his vast strength & seized the gray horse's bit as he plunged by, & fetched him up standing."

It was the work of an instant. But it was an instant that would change Lewis's life. The Elmira *Daily Advertiser* ran stories the following two days telling of serious injury and death from runaway horse accidents. Had Lewis failed to stop the horse they all would likely have been killed.

Twain remembered, "I ran on & on . . . saying to myself, 'I shall see it at the turn of the road; they can never pass that turn alive.' When I came in sight of that turn, I saw two wagons there bunched together—one of them full of people. I said, 'Just so—they are staring petrified at the remains.'

"But when I got amongst that bunch—there sat Ida in her buggy & nobody hurt, not even the horse or the vehicle. Ida was pale but serene. As I came tearing down she smiled back over her shoulder at me & said, 'Well, we're *alive* yet, *aren't* we?' A miracle had been performed—nothing less."

Lewis was immediately hailed as a hero. The next day the family members surprised him with a party in his honor. Twain presented Lewis with a set of autographed books and fifty dollars. Another friend of the family gave him twenty-five dollars. The Cranes gave him the incredible sum of four hundred dollars, and Ida Langdon presented him with a gold watch inscribed "John T. Lewis, who saved three lives at the deadly peril of his own, Aug. 23, 1877. This in grateful remembrance from Mrs. Charles J. Langdon."

Lewis attempted to use the money to pay back part of his debt to the family, but Ida demurred, because she knew that Charles Langdon himself, who was away on a trip, would also want to add to the reward. She was right. Upon his return Langdon gave Lewis a check for a thousand dollars. Lewis was not only debt-free, but the owner, rather than the tenant, of a sixty-four-and-a-half-acre farm.

Later the family also raised money for a modest pension for Lewis after injuries from a life of hard labor made it difficult for him to work on the farm.

As a frequent resident in Elmira, Mark Twain and Lewis became good friends. Writing about Lewis at the time of the incident, Twain remembered, "Lewis . . . is of mighty frame & muscle, stocky, stooping, ungainly, has a good manly face and clear eye. Aged about 45 & the most picturesque of men, when he sits in his fluttering work-day rags, humped forward into a bunch, with his slouched hat mashed over his ears and neck. It is a spectacle to make the broken hearted smile." Twain admired John's wisdom, faith, and integrity, but it was the famous rescue that made a lifelong impression on the great writer. Kermon Thomasson, former editor of *Messenger,* who studied the life of John T. Lewis, insists that there is every reason to think that the character of the runaway slave, Jim, in Twain's novel *The Adventures of Huckleberry Finn,* is based at least in part on Lewis. In the novel every white character tries to take advantage of Huck. Only Jim treats him as a person and loves him for who he is. Twain admired and respected Lewis and may have used him as the model for his hero. If so, it's an important influence that Brethren life and thought had on what many consider the greatest American novel ever written—and another Brethren brush with greatness.

John Lewis became a local celebrity because of his life-saving actions, yet he became a celebrity among the Brethren for quite a different reason. Years before, on September 17, 1862, the Battle of Antietam had been fought near Sharpsburg, Maryland, with the famous Dunker meetinghouse as a backdrop. More Americans were killed in one day in that battle than in any other day of combat in American history.

The true extent of the suffering and misery of the Civil War, by and large, had been shielded from the populace, until photographer Matthew Brady took many photographs of the Antietam battlefield filled with unburied bodies. The effect was electrifying. The display at a gallery in New York revealed a sign of warfare that before had been hidden from the populace.

One of Brady's photographs remains a famous icon to this day: the Brethren meetinghouse shot through with holes from bullets and cannon balls, with the Confederate dead sprawled before it.

It was customary after battles for the soldiers to take items with them as souvenirs. Sergeant Nathan F. Dykman of Company H of the 107th New York regiment stole the Bible from the Brethren meetinghouse.

In 1906 the company met at a reunion in upper New York State to remember the famous battle. Dykman's widow brought the Bible, which he had wanted returned to the church. The members of the company decided it was time to do so. The question was how. There were no Brethren churches anywhere near the area, and no one knew any Brethren— until it was remembered that John Lewis lived nearby.

When the Bible was delivered into his hands, Lewis was photographed with it, and then he shipped it to Sharpsburg, Maryland, after which it was gratefully acknowledged by the church. The church took care of it for many years, but later it was donated to the museum at the site of the battlefield.

Lewis lived the remainder of his life in relative comfort, supported by both his labor and his pension. He loved to receive Brethren magazines, which he read religiously. It was his wish that his funeral service be performed by a Brethren minister, insisting that only the Brethren preached the full gospel and that he did not want another minister to perform the service. The Bible said the sheep would know the proper shepherd, and he didn't recognize other shepherds. "I have tried to be faithful to the New Testament and order of the Brethren," he once wrote.

Lewis died on July 23, 1906, as he was being driven to the hospital by ambulance. The headline of the local paper read, "John T. Lewis, Colored Hero, Dies on Way to Hospital," and a smaller headline identified him as "Only Dunkard in Vicinity." Alas, the minister who was to perform the service was in Iowa at the time, so Lewis's service was conducted by the undertaker. For many years no stone marked his grave until Kermon Thomasson put a proposal before the Brethren Historical Committee, which led to a fund drive that culminated in 2000 with the installation of a simple granite grave marker. The brass plaque reads: John T. Lewis, 1835-1906.

*The One About*

# THE CATTLE QUEEN OF LINCOLN COUNTY WHO WAS PROTECTED BY BILLY THE KID

**SUSAN MCSWEEN BARBER • CA. 1845-1931**

9

*No one knows for sure why Susanna Hummer, an eighteen-year-old Brethren girl from Adams County, Pennsylvania, left home after the Battle of Gettysburg in July of 1863.*

One thing we know for sure is that by the time she died in 1931 under the name Susan McSween Barber, she had become famous as "The Cattle Queen of New Mexico." More important, she was notorious as one of the survivors of the Lincoln County War, made famous in more than two hundred books and many movies for its association with the infamous Billy the Kid.

The famous Civil War battle at Gettysburg took place only a few miles from Susanna's childhood home. Some say she was distraught after the death of her close friend, Jennie Wade, who was the only civilian to die in the conflict when a bullet passed through two wooden doors while she was baking bread for Union soldiers. Others say Susanna fell in love with one of the soldiers—Union or Confederate, I don't know—and jumped out of her bedroom window and ran off. Either way, the daughter of Peter Hummer, a self-described "gentleman farmer" and father of sixteen children, disappeared for ten years before her name appeared on a wedding license.

Attorney Alexander A. McSween, described as a "red-haired Scot with a sweeping mustache," married Susanna on August 23, 1873, in Eureka, Kansas. By this time she was calling herself Sue E. Homer. Susan soon distinguished herself as a canny financial manager, but despite the couple's ambitious plans, a Wall Street panic, the subsequent recession, and a plague of locusts led to their move to southeastern New Mexico.

The McSweens soon became associated with "The House," as the firm of L. G. Murphy and Company was known. "The House" served as a central location for the community and exerted economic control over the region by sending out octopus-like tendrils in all directions, selling supplies to settlers, brokering land, providing banking services, and serving as the saloon as well. Everything in Lincoln went through "The House," with the typically corrupt and carousing, strong-arm ways of the western frontier.

In contrast to her upbringing as one of the "plain people," or perhaps because of it, Susan McSween was known as the best-dressed woman in Lincoln, relying on elaborate makeup and a fancy hair-do. While many people lived in simple houses, known as *jacales*, with blanket flaps for doors, the McSweens lived in a nine-room hacienda that was magnificently furnished and carpeted, with curtains on each window. One Hispanic resident remembered that she "always looked like a big doll." Others described her as "vivacious." She was not popular, however, with either the Anglo or the Hispanic population. She disdained all Catholics and boasted that she was descended from Germanic nobility. Nor did her husband's business practices help. His salary was totally dependent on a percentage of the collections he made on behalf of "the House," and his heavy-handed techniques earned him plenty of enemies.

Things improved for the couple until McSween split with Murphy and "the House" over the estate of a late business partner. In the meantime McSween went into partnership with a young Englishman named John H. Tunstall, then in direct competition with "the House."

In 1878 legal wrangling gave way to gunfire. On February 18 of that year, Tunstall (McSween's new partner) was murdered by associates of Murphy and what became known as the Lincoln County War broke out. The climax came on July 19. Despite the presence of troops from Fort Stanton, no one stopped the McSweens' enemies from pouring oil on their house and setting it aflame.

By the time order was restored, nineteen were dead, including Alexander McSween. Susan escaped as her home was burned to the ground. In the largely fictional accounts that were published later, she supposedly begged for her piano to be spared, a fact she vehemently denied in later days when she referred to "her troubles." Many of her cattle were stolen by her enemies, her possessions were destroyed, and her husband had been murdered.

One of those who escaped the carnage was William Antrim, better known as Billy the Kid, who had fought on the side of the McSweens. As a result the Lincoln County War became the stuff of legend. Dime novels and sensational journalists reduced the Lincoln County War to a battle between good and evil on the frontier, but scholar Kathleen P. Chamberlain, in her article "In the Shadow of Billy the Kid: Susan McSween and the Lincoln County War," suggests that it was more a battle between competing capitalist interests, which smacked of the greed and glamour of the Gilded Age. Order was restored when a new territorial governor, Lew Wallace, was appointed. Wallace was in the midst of writing his famous novel *Ben Hur* and couldn't wait to be posted anywhere other than New Mexico. Thus, Susan McSween experienced a good deal of difficulty when she sought justice and the return of her cattle. She was the target of many accusations, probably false, about her lack of morality, especially in regard to alleged sexual relations. Lawsuits were flung from both sides.

It is a testament to Susan's financial acumen that eventually she recovered much of her cattle, re-established herself as a land baron, and restored her reputation and fortune. She married the attorney George B. Barber and a few years later arranged what seems to have been an amicable divorce.

The Cattle Queen of New Mexico, in the words of Chamberlain, "reinvented herself as a lady." Some recalled her as stingy and parsimonious, while others wrote of her generosity. Photographs show a handsome woman giving the appearance of substance and confidence.

Later in life Susan moved to White Oaks, a town down river from Lincoln, where she lost money in oil drilling. In 1923 she suffered yet another house fire, this time accidental, and escaped by jumping from an upstairs window. A few years later she injured a hip in a fall and began a downward spiral. She died childless on January 3, 1931, still a figure of legend and renown.

One can only speculate about what it was in the Dunker background of Susanna Hummer McSween Barber that led to her becoming one of the legendary figures of the Old West.

# THE INVENTOR OF THE ARTIST'S TABLET THAT SOLD MILLIONS

**DAVID EMMERT • 1854-1911**

## 10

UNITED STATES
PATENT OFFICE

OUT TO
LUNCH

*A few years ago the eminent Brethren historian Donald F. Durnbaugh was giving me a tour of the extensive special collections in the library at Juniata College.* He had just given me a peek into a room that housed shelf after shelf of Christopher Sauer Bibles, a staggering treasure trove. Suddenly he stopped and asked, "Have you ever heard of David Emmert?"

No, truth be told, I hadn't.

David Emmert was one of the first true artists among the Brethren and also one of the first teachers at what would become Juniata College, the first Brethren institution of higher education.

He was the eighth of nine children born to a farm family that lived near what would become the Antietam National Battlefield near Hagerstown, Maryland. David's father was one of the ministers of the congregation that met in the Mumma meetinghouse, known through that battle as the "Dunker Church." The man was against education for his children, believing that it served no useful purpose and, furthermore, could do harm by opening the minds of young people to possibilities in the larger world. In his opinion, reading the Bible and handling money were enough for anyone.

From an early age David Emmert was always drawing, and at the age of three, he had decided that art would be his vocation. He was inspired by everyday things, such as broken plaster, the shadows cast by the firelight, blotches of mud that suggested bigger pictures. Everything had a story. He had come to believe that art was a way of honoring God.

As a child he also witnessed the plight of many children in the area who had been orphaned by both life and the war, and he resolved to help orphans once he became an adult.

David experienced an important turning point in his life when his brother Jonathan, ten years his senior, became one of the first Brethren to graduate from college despite their father's assertion that "I would rather see you dead than get an education." Only a few years later, Jonathan, who had encouraged David to continue painting, died. David Emmert decided it was his task to carry on his brother's work; he got an education of his own and became a teacher.

David had moved to Waynesboro, Pennyslvania, in 1872 and gotten a job with Jacob Zuck, making tools in his workshop. Zuck recognized his employee's genius, and in 1876, when Zuck became one of the founders of what would eventually become Juniata College, he insisted that David Emmert become that institution's art teacher.

In addition to teaching, Emmert created the art for the college catalog, and his sketches of the many buildings in

Huntingdon, Pennsylvania, helped raise money for the school. But it was in 1877 that Emmert created the thing that should have made him very, very famous. He stopped to see a man named J. C. Blair, who ran a stationery store in Huntingdon and had hopes of selling his stationery products across the country. Emmert was interested in getting a notebook for a class he wanted to take at the college. J. C. Blair sold composition books with lined paper, but David wanted something else. So he decided to make it himself right there in the shop.

Emmert took a piece of newsprint and cut it into sheets that were 5 ¾ inches by 8 ½ inches. He stacked the sheets together and nailed some carpet tacks through the paper into a piece of pressed board. He had invented the artist's tablet and didn't even know it.

That tablet still exists today, with Emmert's notes on it. He found he could use the tablet for writing or for sketching ideas that would lead to drawing better pictures. And J. C. Blair discovered that many people wanted tablets just like Emmert's. It wasn't long before he decided to add a paper cover and asked Emmert to design it. The tablet was so popular that it was soon sold everywhere and J. C. Blair's business grew and grew. Emmert's drawing on the cover included a pencil, so Blair had to sell pencils too. When J. C. Blair offered to share the profits from the tablets with Emmert, he said no. He had other things on his mind—the orphans.

The college had been founded at a time when the economy was going through a depression, and there were orphans everywhere. The college students were doing what they could to help them, feeding them and giving them clothes. But the orphans were sometimes housed with the mentally ill, the homeless, and with criminals, who made them the objects of horrible abuse. Other orphans were herded onto trains and shipped west, where some became virtual slaves of the farmers who adopted them. Emmert saw that many of these orphans were themselves growing up to be criminals or mentally ill and realized that his love for the children was even more than his love for teaching art. He put his energies into founding two homes for orphans and helped start a third. He established job positions that we would call caseworkers today, people who worked to establish good matches between families and orphans.

Emmert's artwork attracted the attention of the public to his projects. The drawings were so appealing that readers would turn to his magazines just because of his pictures. At the same time, Emmert's talent also attracted the attention of famous artists who encouraged him to move to Europe where his talent would be appreciated. But there was simply no room in his life for this personal advancement.

Emmert's attempt to balance his love of teaching art (he would teach as many as seven courses simultaneously) with his love of working for the benefit of the orphans left no room for serious artistic endeavors. His home became filled with half-finished canvases. And he deliberately refused raises in salary.

Emmert remained active in the Church of the Brethren, serving as a deacon in his local congregation. A writer as well as an artist, a teacher as well as one who helped orphans, a husband and a father to three sons, he was always busy, always trying to do more in the name of God. Meanwhile, millions of tablets were sold to buyers who filled the pages with art of their own.

Emmert died in 1911 at the age of 56. He was very sick before he died, leaving behind many unfinished paintings. He told his friends that he hoped he would be able to paint pictures in heaven.

In 1976 the United States celebrated its bicentennial. As part of that celebration, the Smithsonian Institution thought that David Emmert's original tablet was such an important invention that they asked to borrow it so it could be displayed at the museum. Oddly, permission was not granted.

# LITTLE MISS SURESHOT

**PHOEBE ANN MOSEY/"ANNIE OAKLEY" • 1860-1926**

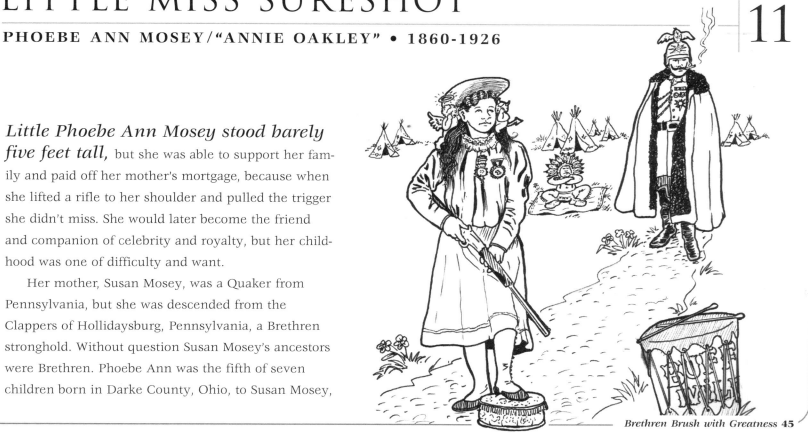

*Little Phoebe Ann Mosey stood barely five feet tall,* but she was able to support her family and paid off her mother's mortgage, because when she lifted a rifle to her shoulder and pulled the trigger she didn't miss. She would later become the friend and companion of celebrity and royalty, but her childhood was one of difficulty and want.

Her mother, Susan Mosey, was a Quaker from Pennsylvania, but she was descended from the Clappers of Hollidaysburg, Pennsylvania, a Brethren stronghold. Without question Susan Mosey's ancestors were Brethren. Phoebe Ann was the fifth of seven children born in Darke County, Ohio, to Susan Mosey, whose husband, Jacob, a veteran of the War of 1812, died when Phoebe Ann was six years old. Susan then married Daniel Brumbaugh, a neighbor of advanced years, who may have been Brethren as well.

Upon Daniel's death, the family plunged deep into poverty. As was common at the time, some of the children were farmed out to other families. For a short period of time, Phoebe Ann lived with a family who treated her so badly that she refused to name them in her autobiography. According to some records, these people were members of the Studebaker family, who also had strong Brethren roots, but this branch may have been Methodist rather than Brethren by this time, as many Studebakers abandoned the Brethren rather than submit to the strict discipline of the group.

By age nine Phoebe Ann was back living at home, helping put food on the table. Her hunting skills became legendary. As mentioned earlier, she paid off her mother's mortgage with the game she shot and sold. Her extraordinary skill with a 22-caliber rifle intersected the path of luck when the renowned marksman Frank Butler (1850-1926) came to town. Phoebe Ann was twenty-one at the time. Butler had a standing bet of $100 (an extraordinary sum for the day) that no one could out-shoot him. Phoebe Ann matched him shot for shot—until Butler missed his twenty-fifth target.

Butler later considered that the luckiest miss of his life. The two went on to share a happy marriage of forty-four years before their deaths within days of each other. At first Phoebe Ann helped Frank with his shooting show, but it soon became obvious who was the best shot. Phoebe Ann, under her stage name Annie Oakley, became the lead name on the marquee. She was renowned for her ability to split a playing card in half edgewise from ninety feet away using her trusty 22-caliber rifle and then peppering it with five or six more holes as it fell to the ground.

Phoebe Ann as Annie Oakley became the stuff of legend. Some of the facts are hard to sort out. Ken Morse, in his book of Brethren stories titled *Preaching in a Tavern* (1997), for instance, states that she was sixteen at the time of her famous contest with Butler, but confusion arose because the pair later changed the year of her birth when a rival female sharp-shooter attracted more attention because she was younger than Annie Oakley.

Sitting Bull gave Annie the nickname "Little Miss Sureshot" when she and Butler traveled with Buffalo Bill's Wild West Show in 1885. Regardless of what she was called, Annie Oakley was the subject of numerous biographies (some almost totally fictional) during her lifetime and the subject of movies, television shows, and the Broadway musical *Annie Get Your Gun.* But, according to Ken Morse, "People who knew [her], as well as her biographers, described her as 'modest,' 'soft-spoken,' 'surprisingly feminine,' 'quiet and sedate,' and even 'puritanical' in her private life."

In 1891 Annie Oakley toured Europe. As part of her act she shot a cigarette out of Butler's mouth. Kaiser Wilhelm asked Oakley to perform the feat on him and she successfully complied, although later she is said to have remarked she didn't like the Kaiser because he looked like the kind who might start a war. After her premonition came true, she informed him that if they repeated the trick she wouldn't guarantee the results.

Annie also became a friend of Pennsylvania governor and Brethren minister Martin Grove Brumbaugh and was a regular guest at his home. One of Brumbaugh's biographers remembered:

> Annie Oakley, the greatest woman marksman who ever lived, regularly saluted him as cousin, because her stepfather was a Daniel Brumbaugh from Hollidaysburg. Mrs. Brumbaugh was a shooting pupil of Annie Oakley at Pinehurst, and Annie and her husband spent several weekends at the Brumbaugh home in Germantown. (Flory 124)

Later in life Annie Oakley suffered railway and auto accidents, both requiring long recoveries, but her skills with the rifle never diminished. Even in her sixties her target shooting amazed audiences. More important, however, she supported many charities and was a champion of women's rights. After she died (her husband stopped eating and died twenty days later), it was discovered that her great fortune had already been spent on the charities that mattered to her.

# THE DUNKER WHO WON THE RACE AND WROTE THE FUTURE

**12**

### MARTIN GROVE BRUMBAUGH • 1862-1930

*Martin Grove Brumbaugh was the premier Brethren educator, the first Dunker to earn a Ph.D.; a professor of pedagogy,* as it was then known; twice president of Juniata College (1895-1906 and 1924-1930); writer, historian, fisherman, minister; school superintendent at both the local and state level. And if that wasn't enough, he was governor of Pennsylvania from 1915 to 1919. He even received nineteen votes at the Republican Convention of 1916 as a dark horse candidate for president.

Here is no accidental Brethren brush with greatness. M. G. Brumbaugh was great in every sense of the word—

so great that when the initial list of characters for this book was put together by the editors he was overlooked. Martin Grove Brumbaugh is a great example of how Brethren fail to honor those who shine in their midst.

Charles Calvert Ellis succeeded Brumbaugh as president of Juniata College. Upon Brumbaugh's death, Calvert delivered a lengthy eulogy cataloging the man's many achievements, lamenting the fact that his own church had ignored him. Ellis began by noting that Brumbaugh "has passed beyond the opportunity for us to honor him, but it might be pertinent to ask what contribution did the church make to him?" Ellis went on to say, "It is a sobering fact that aside from giving him the privilege of making an occasional address at Annual Conference the church in general availed herself but little of his great ability nor gave him any recognition except such as came incidentally because he was made President of one of our church colleges." Ellis concluded by noting, ". . . his own people never even named him for an important position in the church so far as I know." Specifically, Brumbaugh was never called to be moderator of the denomination, nor to serve as chair of any of its boards.

Yet, without question, Brumbaugh was much loved by those who knew him. Stories abound of his humanity and precocity. For example, when Martin was a youngster, the Sunday school of the Brethren congregation at James Creek gave away prizes for those who memorized Bible verses, but one Sunday the eight-year-old Brumbaugh emptied the store by taking up virtually the whole class hour reciting 145 verses and earning every single prize that had been set aside for the whole year!

He was a complex and storied character, remembered as one who loved fishing and occasionally would stretch the size of the fish he caught, but he never exaggerated his golf scores. One friend remembered that he "liked to chain smoke cigars while fishing. He said the smoke kept mosquitoes away. While he bought everything else on a monthly charge account at the local store, he always paid cash for his cigars. He did not want to have any record of how many he smoked."

In his later political campaigns, Brumbaugh would lay great emphasis on his working background. In his campaign literature he wrote, "I was born on a Pennsylvania farm. I have worked on a farm, not as a fad, but because I had to earn my daily bread." Elsewhere he spoke of earning his way through school by working on campus and walking twelve miles home every weekend to help his father with various businesses.

Once when he was seventeen, he helped his father gather twelve hundred logs for use as telegraph polls. When a violent storm scattered them over a great distance, he worked until he recovered every one. And as the story goes, when he ran for county superintendent of schools a year later (he grew a beard, the only time in his life, to look older when he campaigned), a farmer promised him his vote when he learned that he was the same person "who helped his father with the telegraph poles." He won the election by that single vote.

Brumbaugh worked tirelessly to improve the schools of Pennsylvania, insisting that physical education and instruction for manual trades be included in the curriculum. He wrote several books on education theory, as well as five volumes of *Standard Readers.* Although many of the reforms he promised when he ran for governor were blocked by a recalcitrant legislature, he did push through great reforms in the matter of child labor, and he favored worker's compensation, voting rights for women, and road improvements.

Brumbaugh also served as Puerto Rico's first minister of education from 1900 to 1902 at the personal request of President McKinley, after it became an American possession in the wake of the Spanish-American War. In those two years he not only instituted many of the foundations for a modern educational system, but he served as acting president of the island's senate and was active in all aspects of Puerto Rico's administration.

Although he had connections with many prominent people, Martin Grove Brumbaugh continued to support the church. He was an ordained minister, frequently appeared at Annual Conference, and advanced the cause of higher education in the church.

In the eyes of his friends, holding the highest elective office ever attained by a member of the Church of the Brethren may be why he was not more honored. Perhaps it was the cigars, or his membership (at least temporarily) in the Masons, or perhaps his marriage to Flora Parks after the death of his first wife. His campaign literature referred to her to as "a ward of Mr. Brumbaugh, as well as a relative. She is an orphan, and twenty years ago was invited to become a member of the family. She has been a counselor and companion of the children, and the entire family is warmly attached to her."

Perhaps Brumbaugh was slighted because as governor of Pennsylvania he was the titular head of the state militia, which he called up at the onset of the World War I. At that time some Brethren young men were being tortured and even killed in camps for refusing to serve in the military, while the leaders of the church were threatened with arrest and imprisonment on a charge of sedition.

Also, in some ways, Brumbaugh was out of step with the temper of the church at that time. Some would call him a progressive's progressive in a church where the true divide was still between conservatives and fundamentalists. But, ironically, it was his book, *History of the German Baptist Brethren*, written in 1899, identifying the Brethren as a progressive body during their European and colonial days and setting the stage for the "Brethren Service miracle," that may have won both admiration and ire. In writing about the past, he insisted that history could "indicate future activities by the church."

Calvert Ellis agreed when he wrote, "As the pioneer historian of the church he revealed to us that the Church of the Brethren was not born of ignorance but of the refinement of learning as well as devotion, pointing out that the founders of the church came to their convictions on the basis of a thorough study of the word of God, and with the opportunity to profit by the mistakes of others in the earlier Reformation days."

At the church's bicentennial in 1908, Brumbaugh himself wrote: "We began an educated and powerful church. Let us try with all our energies to restore the church to its early and its splendid history. We shall thus best serve our church, best serve the great Head of the church, the Son of God."

Brumbaugh's history, however, was not the inevitable seminal volume that it for decades seemed to be. But it *was* the winner of a race to produce the first Brethren history, a volume that was long overdue, and which may not have been as accurate as it was influential.

In "Martin Grove Brumbaugh, the 'Pioneer Brethren Historian' and His Rivals," Donald F. Durnbaugh tells the exciting story of the competition to utilize the treasure trove of Abraham Harley Cassel's priceless collection of "Brethren-related rare books and unique manuscripts from the eighteenth and nineteenth centuries."

Perhaps the Brethren tendency toward noncreedalism discouraged such literary efforts. Durnbaugh notes that at the 1895 Annual Meeting "at least one voice [Landon West] urged the defeat of the motion [to authorize a history] on the basis that the Bible was the only book the church needed." Nevertheless, as the nineteenth century waned, it seemed to several that it was time for the Brethren to produce a definitive history both to serve Brethren churches and to explain the beliefs and tenets beyond the denomination. The final result was that Brumbaugh . . .

. . . appeared like a hurricane force in the later 1890s. In its course he swept aside previous aspirants to the honor of completing the first substantial Brethren history. This he accomplished in a relatively short period; the actual writing of his pioneer history took him just six months. This was effected on top of all of his concurrent responsibilities as professor of pedagogy at the University of Pennsylvania while continuing as president of Juniata College. At the same time he was busily publishing educational texts and frequently lecturing across the nation. Only a man with the superhuman discipline, energy, and drive of an M. G. Brumbaugh could have mastered this amount of work. (Durnbaugh)

In the words of one of his contemporaries, Brumbaugh believed the first Brethren who "promulgated our doctrines were profound scholars and not ignorant men as some might believe." In the decades following the three-way split of the 1880s, when one of the divisive issues was higher education, Brumbaugh sought to justify the present by proving the first Brethren were progressives in all matters. His history was enormously influential, both at the time and in the ensuing decades, portraying the Brethren as the first denomination in America to hold Sunday schools and run a denominational press, who prized religious liberty and shunned, well, shunning. But, as Durnbaugh put it, "all this is current and valuable history except that it is false."

According to Durnbaugh, Brumbaugh ignored Cassel's attempt to correct historical inaccuracies because he understood that "whoever controls the past in some sense also controls the future."

These points are not made to denigrate the memory of Martin Grove Brumbaugh. His history was wildly successful and deeply influential. Even today one finds those outside the Brethren quoting it as a major source when necessary. Though a dubious achievement, by inventing a past for the Brethren as a progressive denomination in Colonial America, Brumbaugh set the stage at least in part for the Brethren Service miracle of the twentieth century with Heifer Project, Church World Service, CROP, the Brethren Service Commission's work in Europe before and after World War II, Brethren Volunteer Service—and so much more. All these are the children of his hastily written history.

# THE COLLEGE PRESIDENT'S WIFE WHO WENT THROUGH HELL

**13**

## EMMA NICE ELLIS • CA. 1876-N.D.

*First Emma Reed Nice found herself in hell. Then she was in heaven. Then she was plunged into—well, you decide.* You also might ask, Who was Emma Nice? She became the wife of Brethren educator Charles Calvert (C. C.) Ellis (1874-1950), who, one might say, was something of a Brethren celebrity. He was an accomplished preacher and writer, called into the ministry, served congregations, and was a three-time Annual

Conference moderator. After earning his Ph.D. at the University of Pennsylvania in 1907, he taught at Juniata College, where he was president from 1930 to 1943 and president emeritus until his death.

But Emma's brush with greatness wasn't her association with C. C. The year was 1901 (a year before they married). She and a friend were attending the Pan-American Exposition in Buffalo, New York. More than sixty years later, she still remembered in vivid detail that unforgettable day.

On July 24, 1963, Emma Nice Ellis, age 87, sat down with M. R. Zigler for a recorded interview for the purpose, in Zigler's words, of "recording early impressions of Mrs. Ellis about the Church of the Brethren as she remembers them." At one point in the conversation, she mentioned that she considered herself "an old fogy in religion" and lamented the fact that "we used to hear sermons about hell and Satan and different things about the church, but we don't hear a word anymore. And intemperance. If anybody would preach that today church members wouldn't go to church."

When Zigler brought up a book by C. H. Balsbaugh about hell, Emma suddenly admitted, "You know, I've been at that bad place."

Not content to let this provocative statement stand on its own, she said, "I don't want to go back there anymore. A friend of mine and I went to the World's Fair. We had a day that I shall never forget." (Based on her description, her experience actually took place at the Pan-American Exposition, even though she remembered the event as the World's Fair.)

> You know we went into a side show where heaven and hell were advertised. We went in there. They put us in a cage and it seemed that we had gone down thousands of miles into the earth and rocks were falling around us. I commenced to cry and Mary didn't and then the one that was taking us down there said, "Don't be afraid." But I couldn't help it. They opened the cage and we got out and there was hell. The man Satan was pulling people in. [*Emma laughed.*] You know. I still cried. I didn't know when he would come near me. Goodness me, it was hard! And then I was just so glad

when we got out. That wasn't the end. Then came heaven after that. Heaven was wonderful. [*She laughed again.*] We walked right out on the street.

Hell and Heaven were part of a midway attraction called "Darkness and Dawn." According to the official program, for twenty-five cents visitors were exposed to . . .

A realistic representation of a departed spirit, whose life on earth has not been exemplary. The visitor witnesses the punishment meted out to scandal-mongers, umbrella borrowers, and other offenders. After the seas of fire are passed, beautiful scenes to delight the eye appear, so that the visitor may be accustomed to the more familiar places above ground.

Had this been her only memory of the day, it's unlikely Emma would have brought it up, but this was September 6, 1901, and Emma and her companion decided they would also try to meet the president.

Well, that wasn't all. I thought we had had about enough. We thought we would go over and see President McKinley who was visiting the exposition that day. We went over there and got into the building where he was shot and saw the whole thing.

At this point Zigler interrupted. "Saw him shot?" he asked. And Emma continued . . .

Yes. Right there in the building in the Temple of Music he was shot. Of course, there were probably two dozen or more people ahead of us. But we saw how the man had his hand wrapped up. We thought nothing of that. But then the shot rang out. And the cursing went on. Outside, around the building and everywhere—oh, I thought I couldn't live over it. Then we went down to the hospital where he was. We thought it so strange, the day before, he was riding around in an open car. I thought the man figured he couldn't get a good shot at him there so it happened in the Temple of Music. Of course they carried the president out and roped us in there for our names and other information. Then I said to Mary, "I'll have to go home now." She said, "I will, too." It was an awful day. I'll never forget it.

Zigler asked, "You heard the shot, did you?"

I saw it. I saw the man. There were about ten or twelve people ahead of us. They grabbed the assassin and put him away. And then they took President McKinley to an ambulance. They took the names of all the people in that line.

Emma recalled that McKinley had been shaking hands with people and that she had not yet come to the front of the line before he was shot.

That was an awful experience. Terrible. Terrible! I never knew how I felt or anything. [*Emma paused.*] So! Eighty-seven years have brought some experiences and they come back to me. But that was one of the saddest ones. You know, the day before he was riding around in an open car. He wasn't afraid. I don't remember about the guards around him. When we got back Charlie said, "I knew you would come home. You couldn't stand that." I've had some little experience in life.

The Charlie she referred to was her future husband.

McKinley died a few days later at the home of John G. Milburn, president of the Pan-American Exposition. The assassin's name was Leon Czolgosz, an anarchist who was later executed for the crime.

# THE MOST FAMOUS, BEST KNOWN BRETHREN POEM EVER

**14**

**MYRA BROOKS WELCH • 1878-1959**

*Back in the era before the Internet and the flood of endless forwards that clog our mailboxes, cute stories, inspiring poems, and urban myths used to be reproduced as smudgy photocopies or messy mimeos,* or even written out with pen and ink and then passed from hand to hand.

When we see the stern expressions of old Dunker portraits, the men with their long white beards, the women in their prayer coverings, the first thought that comes to our minds is probably not "poet." But that's exactly what our ancestors in the faith were. The early Brethren, in fact, were great hymn writers, prolific poets who expressed a deep, mystical, emotional strain in meter and rhyme. It is said that the Solingen Brethren, who were imprisoned in Europe for their faith, wrote more than four hundred hymns during their confinement. Alexander Mack, Jr., son of the first minister among the Brethren, wrote hundreds of poems and hymns, of which only a few were published in English translation, many no longer accessible to modern-day Brethren.

Poems have regularly appeared on the pages of *The Gospel Messenger* and *The Primitive Christian,* and *Family Companion,* along with the many other periodicals published by the Brethren. Some of these were published anonymously, others identified only by initials, but eventually it became acceptable for a Brethren to publish poems under his or her own name.

Still other poems were read and loved by only a few people, occasionally clipped and stuffed between the pages of a Bible and largely forgotten. The Most Famous, Best Known Brethren Poem Ever, however, was written in English. Moreover, you can find it everywhere, because it has been reprinted hundreds of times, often with the ascription "Anonymous," despite the fact that when it was first published it appeared with the author's name. Perhaps this was because it was so instantly popular that people memorized it, copied it by hand, and thumbtacked it on bulletin boards, leading others to copy it as well.

It's been set to music on several occasions, read on the floor of Congress, made the subject of a film, and recited from memory by many who have been touched by its simple, biblical truth.

The Most Famous, Best Known Brethren Poem Ever was included as part of the *New York Times* anthology *The Best Loved Poems of the American People.* It has been the subject of sermons, reprinted in salvation tracts, and probably been read by more people than any other piece of writing by any brother or sister in the three-hundred-year history of the Church of the Brethren.

On one occasion the author's son, Dwight, was sitting on a dais at a YMCA convention in Hawaii when a speaker quoted the poem and lamented that no one knew who had written it. The son was able to rise up and announce that the author was his mother—Myra Brooks Welch.

Myra Brooks Welch was born October 12, 1877, near Bushnell in McDonough County, Illinois. Her mother, Mary Ellen Eshelman Brooks, was Brethren, and her father, John Wesley Brooks, was probably Presbyterian. The family moved to Nebraska and eventually Myra attended McPherson College.

In 1899 the family moved to Oregon, where Myra married Otis Welch in 1901. They had three children, one of whom died at an early age. The family eventually moved to La Verne, California, so the children could attend the college there.

Myra grew up playing musical instruments. She was not only a talented pianist and guitarist but played organ for her church. However, when she was only thirty-five, "old Mr. Arthritis moved into our home." She was confined to a wheelchair, her hands so crippled that she was unable to play an instrument. So she made a different kind of music—with words instead of notes. Unable to hold a pencil in the normal manner, she held one in each hand between her gnarled fingers, tapping the keys with the erasers, telling the "story of an old violin considered worthless until it was played by a master musician" (Morse).

Myra Brooks Welch wrote "The Touch of the Master's Hand" after hearing an inspirational speaker early in 1921. By her account it took her around half an hour to write it. Since her byline was already familiar to readers of *The Gospel Messenger,* she sent this poem in as well, where it was published in the February 26, 1921, issue, earning her seventy-five cents. It's worth remembering that in those days seventy-five cents actually bought something! Still, until the copyright ran out and The Most Famous, Best Known Brethren Poem Ever became part of the public domain, it never earned more than twenty dollars in royalties. The most recent Brethren Press edition, *The Story Behind the Touch of the Master's Hand*, was published in 1997.

Myra's poem took on a life of its own, soon appearing in many different magazines and books, often without her name attached. She made no effort to identify herself as the author, but three different events finally rescued her poem from anonymity. The first happened in 1936, the aforementioned incident at which her son Dwight was presiding at a YMCA meeting in Hawaii when a speaker closed his address with what he thought was an anonymous poem.

Later Myra's father called in to a radio station after the family heard it read aloud on a car radio. And finally, in 1936 the *New York Times Book Review* actively searched for the author. "Myra Brooks Welch included the poem in two of her three poetry collections. The first and third anthologies, published in 1941 and 1957, both took as their title *The Touch of the Master's Hand.*

The author often received visitors from around the world who came to tell her how much the poem meant to them. On one occasion a missionary from India told her that after reading the poem aloud on a troop ship during World War II she and another missionary spent the rest of the day copying the poem by hand over and over at the request of the soldiers.

"The Touch of the Master's Hand" was read aloud on *The Smothers Brothers Comedy Hour,* included in collections by Norman Vincent Peale as well as in *Chicken Soup for the Soul,* and has been the subject of more than one painting.

Myra's poetry in general has been described as "simple and unaffected" (*The Christian Century,* December 3, 1941); "inspiring . . . a needed antidote for present-day cynicism" (*The International Journal of Religious Education,* January 1942); "not great poetry; but sweet and wholesome" (*The Christian-Evangelist,* February 26, 1942); "rather trite and well-worn" (*The Christian Advocate,* January 10, 1946). None of her poems has achieved success anything like the success of "The Touch of the Master's Hand."

One Brethren writer said of her that "she understands the secret of turning dis-appointments into his-appointments. And this secret you may find disclosed in her poems" (Gilbert 19).

# THE BRETHREN COVER GIRL

## ANNA EVANS WILSON • 1881-1928

**15**

*Most of us, perhaps, don't think "cover girl" when we think Brethren, but there's one Brethren cover girl who has brought nothing but happiness* to thousands of folks who have bought the book that she adorns. For people who live beyond the Brethren circle, she may have the best known Brethren face.

This young woman has an expression every bit as intriguing as the Mona Lisa—and a lot more satisfying because there's nothing but good cooking behind it. As we plain folks have been known to put it, "Kissing wears out. Cooking don't." Her face may not have launched a thousand ships, but she has graced thousands of tables with the good things of life.

She's the Inglenook Girl!

At the start of the twentieth century, the Brethren published *The Inglenook,* a magazine that stood for "material and spiritual progress." It cost a dollar a year, paid in advance, but subscribers received a bonus gift: the *Inglenook Cook Book,* which was worth, according to advertisements, a dollar all by itself.

Printed in 1901 and revised in 1911, the *Inglenook Cook Book* has sold more than 100,000 copies, making it the Brethren bestseller. There is nothing in the least bit ironic about this. Even with an active denominational press, Brethren have probably been better known for eating than for writing.

During the summer of 1974, I traveled with a group of La Verne College students who covered 17,500 miles in 84 days presenting a play by Vernard Eller about Brethren origins. We traveled coast to coast, visiting Annual Conference in Roanoke, Virginia; National Youth Conference in Glorieta, New Mexico; several Brethren camps; Bethany Theological Seminary; all six Brethren colleges; and more than fifty congregations. We observed many different theologies, from the Virginia pastor who was sure we were living under our last American president to the western congregation engaged in a heated battle over which brand of vitamins was most Christlike.

The one thing Brethren across the country all had in common was great cooking. From Modesto and Wenatchee in the West to congregations in the heartlands of Virginia, Maryland, Pennsylvania, and everywhere in between, we were given our fill. By the time we returned home our clothes did not fit.

In more than three decades since that journey, I can truthfully say that I've seen far more copies of the *Inglenook Cook Book* than *The Brethren Encyclopedia* in Brethren homes.

Despite the popularity of the cookbook, the identity of the woman on the cover remained unknown for decades. Intrigued by that fact, Kermon Thomasson, then editor of *Messenger,* asked for help in discovering her identity in the November 1984 issue. In the "Page One" column of the February 1985 issue, he describes what happened next:

It wasn't long before letters started arriving. A few offered speculation that proved wrong. But on November 7, I got a letter from Lula M. Carrier Henderson, of Perkins, Okla., telling me that "Miss Inglenook" was her cousin, according to what her mother had always said. In a few days another letter came, from Rena Neff Wright, of Nokesville, Va., substantiating Mrs. Henderson's claim with photocopied pages of a book about the Carrier family.

Letters began to flow back and forth. In December I got a phone call from Beth Wilson, of Torrance, Calif. Her husband, Steven Wilson, is a great-grandson of "Miss Inglenook." And through Mrs. Wilson, I got in telephone contact with Ellen Wilson Sanner, of Placerville, Calif., 81-year-old daughter of "Miss Inglenook" herself!

So now the story can be told: "Miss Inglenook" was Anna Evans Wilson.

Anna's grandfather William Henry Carrier was from Rockingham County, Va. He and his wife, Sarah, eventually settled in Missouri. Their daughter Susan Rebecca married Richard Evans, and they were the parents of Anna, our model.

Why or how Anna came to be on that book cover, even her last surviving child, Ellen, was unable to tell me. Anna married a Baptist man, Samuel Wilson, and joined his faith. They wound up in Oakland, Calif. Anna died relatively young, November 10, 1928, and is buried in Oakland's Mountain View Cemetery.

Ellen Sanner, far removed from the Church of the Brethren world, was astonished to learn that her mother, gone more than half a century, had made the *Messenger* cover. Yes, she remembered the Brethren—"Dunkards, we called them," she chuckled. But she was surprised to learn that the cookbook is still in print, and has always been one of Brethren Press' hottest items. And guess what, Ellen still has her mother's copy of that bestseller!

Mystery solved. And remember, even better than a Brethren brush with greatness is a brush for buttering a platter of hot rolls as they emerge steaming from the oven.

# 16 | A THIRTY-PERCENT TITHER AND MORE

**LAURA WINE • 1899-1969**

*Take plague-bearing rats, a highly infectious disease, a best-selling, alien-abductionist, ghost-story author, white-coated lab researchers who start dying,* and a plague that threatens not just a distant continent but, thanks to air travel, much of the First World, and what do you get? *The Andromeda Strain?*

Not exactly.

Add a faithful Brethren missionary to Nigeria, and what you get is *Fever!*

To the outside world, Brethren missionary Laura Wine is recognized for being the first person known to have contracted and died from Lassa Fever, one of many deadly diseases in Africa. This led to her inclusion in a major bestseller, published in 1974, which may have exposed more people to the Church of the Brethren than any writings by Brethren authors (with the exceptions, perhaps, of the *Inglenook Cook Book* and "The Touch of the Master's Hand").

The book in question, *Fever!*, was written by John G. Fuller, author, documentarian, and playwright, who wrote several bestsellers and won an Emmy Award as a television producer.

Fuller begins his narrative with the following paragraph:

> Although she was used to being wakened at any time of night, the rap on the door shortly after three in the morning on Sunday, January 19, 1969, brought Laura Wine to the realization that the pain in her back was worse. With some effort she fumbled for her flashlight and shined it through the thick canopy of her mosquito netting. Assured there were no African vipers lurking on the cement floor, she parted the netting, tapped her slippers upside down to dislodge any scorpions that might be inside, and put them on. (11)

What follows is a tale of medical intrigue. Fuller describes in vivid detail the primitive nature of the mission outpost, Laura Wine's background, John and Esther Hamer who are also part of the compound, and the story of what brought the Brethren to such an isolated place.

> When the Lassa mission station was founded in the 1920s, an incredulous British officer asked the first Church of the Brethren missionaries: "Why on earth have you chosen this place?" The reply was: "Because there are people there." (Fuller 21)

The author gives a thumbnail sketch of the missionary's life and then proceeds to tell a gripping tale of the onset of a mysterious disease that does not respond to normal treatments. Laura's condition worsens, and a harrowing journey follows as the Hamers drive her across treacherous terrain to a waiting flight that is every bit as dangerous as it sounds.

With a novelist's eye, the countryside is described in detail, as are the conditions in the hospitals. Though heroic efforts keep Laura alive until her arrival in Jos, she continues to fail.

She is failing as the Sunday morning services begin. As "A Mighty Fortress Is Our God" is sung, Laura says without opening her eyes, "Oh, I'm so glad the hymns are in English today!" Since in Lassa the hymns were sung in another language, Laura must have realized that she had been moved. That leads her to ask, "But where am I?"

Those proved to be her final words. She is anointed and receives the laying on of hands, but dies that evening, thousands of miles from her home.

Laura Wine died of Lassa Fever, a disease endemic in West Africa. According to the Centers for Disease Control, between 100,000 to 300,000 contract the virus every year and around 5,000 die. The actual figures are hard to determine, but it is now known that the disease is carried by rats. If humans ingest food that has come in contact with rats or if the dust from rat feces becomes airborne, it is possible for humans to become infected. And humans can spread Lassa Fever among each other. In fact, a nurse in Jos cut her finger while gardening and contracted the disease while swabbing out Laura Wine's mouth.

Fuller's narrative describes how early victims were flown to researchers at Columbia University, but the pathogen was so fatal that research was shut down after a lab assistant and two nurses died of it. Eventually an isolation laboratory, typically associated with a bad science fiction movie, was developed in Atlanta, and some progress against the disease was made. An antiviral drug called Ribavirin proved to be effective much of the time, especially when it was administered early in the course of the disease.

Throughout the narrative Fuller expresses his amazement and admiration for the Brethren missionaries, and missionaries in general, even though he admits he does not share their zeal. The strange thing is that this particular author would choose to tackle such a serious—and dangerous—subject. John G. Fuller (1913-1990) was the author of fourteen books, most of which were tied to the supernatural or to UFOs and alien abductions, books like *The Interrupted Journey,* which tells the story of a couple who claimed to have been abducted by a UFO for medical and scientific experiments and became the foundation of a whole genre. *The Ghost of Flight 401* tells the story of purported ghostly events that followed the tragic crash of an Eastern Air Lines flight in December of 1972. Both were made into TV movies.

Although Fuller had read about Lassa Fever the year before, it was not until 1971, while working on a documentary in Africa on a totally unrelated subject, that Fuller learned about a local outbreak of Lassa Fever. This led him to visit many of the sites associated with Laura Wine as he delved deeper and deeper into the story. In the afterword of *Fever!,* Fuller admits to a great deal of fear as he did his research, leading him at one point to decide he had learned enough, even though researching further outbreaks might have provided him with more information.

During his research for the book, Fuller visited the illustrator of this book, Kermon Thomasson, and his wife, Margaret, in Nigeria where they were serving as missionaries. Kermon owned—and owns—an impressive collection of books about Nigerian and West African history. After Fuller discovered Thomasson's library, he spent most of the rest of his time there, poring over the books and making extensive notes for his book. He failed to give credit where credit was due, but Kermon remembers that Fuller kept saying over and over again, "You've got the damnedest library. You've got the damnedest library."

As it was, Laura Wine came to the attention of the world through the manner of her death. At the time of her passing, the custom of naming diseases after the first person who was diagnosed with them had given way to naming them after the region in which they were first discovered.

But Brethren have always sought to be known less for the manner of their death and more for the manner of their living. And among the Brethren, Laura Wine was no exception. She was one of those "who were poured out like an offering" and have "run the good race." Laura Wine was born in Mount Sidney, Virginia. After receiving a B.S.E. degree from East Radford Teacher's College in Virginia, she earned her nurse's diploma from Bethany Hospital School of Nursing in Chicago.

It had been her dream to serve in the Chinese mission field, especially after coming to know Chinese at both Bethany Theological Seminary and First Church of the Brethren in Chicago. However a history of tuberculosis disqualified her from mission work for health reasons. Consequently, she worked as a school nurse in Oak Park, Illinois, and eventually headed the entire nursing program for the school system. As if that were not enough, she then worked weekends at Bethany Brethren Hospital on Chicago's West Side, an impoverished area of the city that was fraught with danger. According to one story, she was attacked by a mugger, but beat him off and then went on her way to work.

According to a nurse who worked with Laura at Bethany Hospital, no one worked as hard as Laura Wine. She was also impressed at how diligently Laura supported the programs of Chicago First Church, an interracial congregation that was ahead of its time. The support included a thirty-percent tithe, which got her into frequent trouble with IRS officials who found it hard to believe she gave so much of what was not a large salary to her church.

An article in *The Gospel Messenger* upon her departure to Africa in 1964 mentioned that she had only retired from the school system because of mandatory age limits, but that she had decided, at the age of sixty-five, to serve as an unpaid volunteer in Nigeria, which meant that her health history evidently was no handicap.

She was modestly quoted in the article, "I do not really feel any pride in giving what's left—just what's left over!"

Once there Laura proved to be a tireless worker, described by a fellow missionary as "one of the most selfless persons I know. It was simply her way of life to think of others."

Despite her admitted difficulty with both the Hausa and Margi languages (according to one source, the fact that she couldn't master the languages made her feel, at least to some extent, as if she weren't "a real, sure enough missionary"), she considered her work in Africa "the greatest thing in her life" and exhibited "real joy" in her work. Even after her two-year term as a volunteer ended, she did not retire but signed on for another term.

Dr. John Hamer, who accompanied her on that futile flight to save her life, wrote, "Laura Wine's giving of her life, which she was totally prepared to do for the sake of Christian service and medical advancement, was a symbol of love. Love made the difference all the way for her. It was love that made death as easy for her as it had been easy to give her life in service."

# THE DUNKER WHO REALLY HAD THE WHOLE WORLD IN HIS HANDS

## 17

### ANDREW W. CORDIER • 1901-1975

*Andrew Wellington Cordier was a graduate of Manchester College* (1922); he earned his M.A. (1923) and his Ph.D. (*magna cum laude,* 1926) at the University of Chicago; he also studied at the Graduate Institute of International Studies in Geneva, Switzerland.

Born on a farm near Canton, Ohio, he later attributed his work ethic to the long hours he spent working with his parents, beginning at the age of five. He was quarterback of his high school football team, and throughout his life he drew upon the athletic stamina developed during those years.

Cordier was first licensed and then ordained by the Church of the Brethren. He was an influential churchman, a visible presence at Annual Conference, and an active supporter of the church's ministries.

Cordier was the chair of the Department of History and Political Science at Manchester College from 1925 to 1944 and a lecturer for Indiana University's Extension Division. He also helped establish the first peace studies program at the college level—anywhere. A world traveler, he saw many of the world's trouble spots firsthand. As a teacher he inspired many of his students to accomplish great things in their careers.

He accepted the call to become the first chair of the Brethren Service Commission in 1942 and served for three years during that crucial time in our history. He was instrumental in opening up the work of the Brethren in Puerto Rico.

If Andrew Cordier had simply retired in 1944 he would still be remembered as one of the greatest and most influential Brethren of all time. However, at this point in his life, he entered the larger world of international diplomacy, taking a position in the State Department as World War II waned. It was becoming clearer that the Allies would win the war against the Axis. The question was whether the nations of the world could win the peace. The failure of the League of Nations after World War I was recognized as one of the factors that led to the ruinous conflict that was ending.

One reason for that failure was the United States' refusal to join the League of Nations. There was talk about a new organization to replace the old, one that would have more of an impact. Cordier, in his capacity as an expert on international security, directly helped shape this new organization and was one of those who influenced the government of the United States to support and join what became the United Nations.

Then he became one of the UN's principal movers and shakers. Cordier was assistant to the secretary-general and then under-secretary of the United Nations from 1944 to 1962. His commitment to peace stood him well in his tireless work for negotiation and reconciliation. A few years after he left the UN, Cordier told *Messenger,* "I feel . . . that if the UN had not existed, we could have had World III several times in the last twenty-five years." He spoke of the way the United Nations put out what he called "brush fires" that could have led to major international conflagrations.

Cordier was known for his extraordinary endurance, allowing him to work what seemed to others as impossible hours. His tireless preparation would pay off as he worked with contending parties to find places of middle ground and agreement. He was endlessly patient. His work would sometimes find him in quiet consultation. On other occasions he would be in the midst of physically dangerous confrontations in trouble spots around the world.

As an example, once when the Korean War was raging and neither the Soviets nor the United States were talking, he managed to get Dean Rusk, assistant secretary of state for Far Eastern Affairs, and Yakov A. Malik, the representative of the Soviet Union to the UN, to come to the clubroom in his basement to talk things out, reviving communication between the two countries.

His prodigious memory made him the perfect parliamentarian for the organization. He could quote from the charter and other relevant documents without having to look them up, and once, when the organization was stuck on a point and he himself was sick and asleep at home, he was awakened with a phone call asking for direction on an obscure parliamentary point. Cordier was able to quote "chapter and verse for the precise rule to resolve the argument."

He could work for hours with warring parties without ever tiring. He was also a personable and much loved employer, personally supervising the 3,500 employees of the United Nations. The staff came from the four corners of the earth, but he maintained a positive attitude among the workforce.

Cordier adapted his style to suit the needs of the people with whom he worked. Under Trygve Lie, the first secretary-general of the United Nations, he was called upon for a good deal of advice. Lie's successor, Dag Hammarskjöld, preferred to make his own decisions, so Cordier excelled at executing those decisions.

In his address lauding Cordier when he was awarded an honorary doctor of divinity degree by Bethany Theological Seminary, Dr. Donald F. Durnbaugh called the United Nations "this imperfect indispensable institutionalized hope for a more secure world."

Cordier, speaking to *Messenger* on the twenty-fifth anniversary of the United Nations, emphasized the need for hope. "I think hope and reality ought to go hand in hand," he said. "Your hopes cannot be realized unless you work for them. And you cannot work for them effectively unless you start where the starting point is, so to speak, and then move forward. Then your hopes become realized."

Cordier was a familiar figure on television, sitting to the left of every Assembly president throughout those years. He would sometimes whisper advice without being noticed to help the various leaders who relied on him for guidance.

He brought the same spirit of reconciliation to his life in the church, serving as a vice president of the National Council of Churches of Christ in the USA, and as a member of the Commission of International Affairs for both the National and World Councils of Churches. He was named to represent both the Protestant and Orthodox churches as part of a delegation to greet Pope Paul VI on his trip to the United States. And he remained active in the Church of the Brethren as a speaker and leader.

Cordier resigned his UN post in 1962, when the Soviets accused him of trying to run the United Nations by himself. He chose not to make himself the issue and instead moved back into the life of an academic, taking the position of dean of the School of International Affairs at Columbia University. He told one reporter that he expected to find his return to the academic world "less fascinating" than the world of international conflict and crisis he had left behind. Soon he had moved the school into a brand new fifteen-story building.

Six years later Cordier found himself acting president of the university. At that time the United States seemed to be falling apart at the seams. Riots, assassinations, social unrest, a deteriorating war in Vietnam were all part of a general breakdown in society. College campuses were a microcosm of society as an active and sometimes violent student movement closed down some campuses and paralyzed others. A student strike at Columbia shut down many parts of the university and led to a violent police charge and the arrests of hundreds of students, alienating the faculty, administrators, and many thousands more of the student body from the president, Grayson Kirk. Columbia's embattled president resigned and Cordier reluctantly took over.

Using the same skills he employed at the UN, Cordier reached out to all members of the student community. He was tough enough to effect the arrests of a very few, but he worked hard to incorporate all the populations of the university into a process of reconciliation. He invited hundreds of students, faculty, and community members into his home for dinner and discussions and soon made peace among warring factions. He also reached out to and included the largely African-American community that surrounded the university.

Cordier continued to work in the academic, political, and Christian worlds until his death in 1975. He was nominated for the Nobel Peace Prize in 1973. He and his wife, Dorothy Butterbaugh of North Manchester, were married in 1924 and had two children. The auditorium at Manchester College was named in his honor, and it is in North Manchester that the two are buried.

# *THAT* TRIAL OF THE CENTURY

**NATHAN LEOPOLD • 1904-1971**

## 18

*It was the Trial of the Century. Not that there haven't been several "trials of the century"!* Some would say Joe Hill's trial (1914), or the trial of Sacco and Vanzetti (1921), or the Scopes Monkey trial (1925) qualifies as the trial of the twentieth century. Others would point to the media circus that surrounded the O. J. Simpson trial (1994-95), which certainly helped invent the court genre on cable and mainstream television.

But there was a time when the names Leopold and Loeb were at the center of a media circus, which was little less than the perfect storm. They were famous—infamous—for all the wrong reasons, and the outrage that followed their famous lawyer's success at wrangling sentences of life-plus-99-years for the two spoiled geniuses, instead of the gallows as demanded by the populace, sold all the newspapers that anyone could desire.

Both Leopold and Loeb were Jewish in a nation where anti-Semitism was not only strong, but socially accepted. Their religion, their wealth, their arrogance (they viewed themselves as supermen who could commit the perfect crime), and their famous lawyer, Clarence Darrow, all contributed to a media frenzy that was every bit as fierce as what we observe today in an era of twenty-four-hour-news stations and court TV.

Darrow argued that there was something essentially wrong with the two young men, that they were the victims of their own genetics, that there was a flaw in their personalities that led to the murder and that, in a certain sense, they were not responsible for their acts. Darrow was smart enough to argue the trial before a judge instead of a jury, and after a twelve-hour summation, which some consider the speech of Darrow's life, the verdict of life-plus-99-years was handed down.

Following the sensational thrill murder in 1924 of an innocent boy who had a chisel driven through his head, the crime, the trial, and the imprisonment led to books, films, and endless ruminations over the years. And the trial was still fresh enough in the memory of both the public and the media when 33 years, 275 days, and 18 hours after the verdict was handed down, Nathan Leopold stepped out of prison into parole—and into the custody of the Church of the Brethren in Castañer, Puerto Rico. The year was 1958.

During his imprisonment Leopold had exhibited every sign of change. He learned twelve more languages (he already knew fifteen) and became an accomplished X-ray technician. He organized correspondence courses for prisoners in nineteen different prisons, established a library and educational classes in his own prison, taught himself Braille so he could tutor a blind prisoner, learned pharmaceutical skills, and volunteered as a medical guinea pig, putting himself at great risk to help scientists study dangerous diseases such as malaria.

So great was the apparent change that W. Harold Row, executive secretary of the Brethren Service Commission, and other Brethren lobbied for several years for his parole. Row had obtained the cooperation of the governor of Puerto Rico so that Leopold could work in Castañer, technically part of the United States but far from the media and the public eye.

With the support of celebrities, including the poet Carl Sandburg, Leopold's parole was finally granted. (His partner, Richard Loeb, had been murdered in prison many years before. Though sensational rumors about the murder circulated for decades, it seems likely that it was prearranged because Loeb had ceased to use his personal wealth to buy luxuries for some of the other prisoners.)

That the Brethren were in Puerto Rico at all was something of a historical accident. In an aborted attempt to send a unit of conscientious objectors consisting of medical personnel to China (right-wing columnist Westbrook Pegler inflamed the prejudice against COs), the Brethren unit began a crash course in Spanish and was soon on its way to Puerto Rico, which as a commonwealth of the United States was exempt from the hastily passed legislation that kept the COs on American soil.

The unit was named after Martin Grove Brumbaugh because he had a great reputation in Puerto Rico years before as the first commissioner for education and drastically revamped the education system. Having the name Brumbaugh helped the Brethren as they attempted to establish a hospital in isolated Castañer.

Leopold's work in Puerto Rico was a great success. After working as an X-ray technician at the hospital, he remained on the island and engaged in research in the spread of diseases, working on novel ways of tracking the transmission of intestinal parasites. He published scientific work on his research as well as a book on the birds of Puerto Rico. (Leopold had amassed an amazing collection of birds while a teenager, and his collection was donated to the Audubon Museum in Elgin, Illinois, before his trial.)

Years after his release from parole, Leopold remained a friend of the Brethren. During a visit to the offices of the General Board in Elgin in 1964, he made this comment: "My only criticism is that you Brethren hide your light under a bushel. You are too quiet. Nobody knows about the Brethren and they need to know. In today's kind of world, I think you have a positive duty to make your witness known. You owe the world more than blankets and food; you owe an example. Don't be quite so retiring; give up a trifle of your reserve for the sake of the world."

Leopold later wrote: "So far as I am aware, mine was the first case in which the Brethren sponsored a man released from prison on parole. To me the Brethren Service Commission offered the job, the home, and the sponsorship without which a man cannot be paroled. But it gave me so much more than that—the companionship, the acceptance, the love which would have rendered a violation of parole almost impossible. A man would have had to work hard indeed to violate parole in such an environment."

There were skeptics, however, who insisted that Leopold took advantage of the Brethren good nature and violated his parole with regularity, traveling all over the island against regulations, purchasing liquor, and failing to return by the time of his curfew. In response to these stories, some Brethren jumped to his defense. One of those was Marie Brubaker, who wrote: "I remember him as one who tried as hard as anyone I've known, struggling against tremendous odds, to atone for the wrongs he was guilty of doing. I felt he loved God and his neighbor. I'm thankful that the Church of the Brethren dared to act on what we believe. I'm willing to leave my friend where I am sure he is—in God's hands and heart."

Another Brethren, Lena Willoughby, traveled with her husband, Dr. William G. Willoughby, and Nathan Leopold on a trip through Europe. She remembered him as a charming, intelligent man. Reflecting on the loss the world might have suffered had he been executed decades before, she wrote, "When Nate died, I grieved for him as a friend, a friend who was sensitive to my humanness but without judgment, a friend who knew my limitations but believed in my worth, a friend who could soften hopelessness because he himself had not despaired. What could society have gained through the death of such a man? Nothing except vengeance and waste!"

As long as he lived Leopold was a lightning rod. He served as an example for those who argued against the death penalty and as an example of what true rehabilitation could accomplish, yet he was the touchstone for those who argued that he proved that clever and influential people could beat—and cheat—the justice system and that his freedom was a slap in the face to his victim.

On one occasion Leopold suggested to the Willoughbys that his prior behavior was predetermined, quoting the behaviorist B. F. Skinner, and that to a certain extent his crime was inevitable. The Brethren offered the chance to the former murderer to continue his transformation, however, and offered him the love and acceptance that is almost impossible to imagine—the same sort of love that Christians claim God displayed through the cross.

# THE ACCIDENTAL INVENTION

**19**

## ROY J. PLUNKETT • 1910-1994

*You can't always get what you want, you don't always get what you need, but you sometimes find what you weren't looking for,* and that can be better than anything you imagined. And you just might be lucky that you didn't get blown up!

On April 6, 1938, at DuPont's Jackson Laboratory in Deepwater, New Jersey, Roy J. Plunkett was working with refrigeration gases. It was his first assignment with the company. Freon was used in refrigeration, and Plunkett was investigating its properties when he and his assistant, Jack

Rebok, made a mistake. They opened a cylinder of the gas but it failed to discharge as expected, so it was laid aside. Later the assistant thought that the cylinder weighed too much even though the normal assumption would have been that the Freon had somehow leaked away. Plunkett shook the cylinder, weighed it, and, deciding to risk the danger of an explosion, cut it open. They discovered that the Freon had undergone a chemical change. The assistant turned the tube upside down and nothing came out. Plunkett discovered that, as he put it in his lab journal, "A white solid material was obtained. . . ."

That discovery was PTFE or polytetrafluoroethylene, better known as Teflon (the trademark name that has long since expired), a substance that has become a part of everyday life and language. After the substance was subjected to a variety of tests, it was discovered that it didn't react with chemicals, that it maintained its integrity whether the temperature was 500 degrees above zero or 400 degrees below, that it withstood the pressures of vacuum, making it perfect for use in space, and that it was a perfect insulator.

At first, from 1941 to 1948, its use was limited to defense work. Teflon first achieved public awareness when it was used on frying pans in France. Now over half a billion pots and pans have been sold because of its amazing no-stick quality. It has since been used to coat electrical wires, light bulbs, chemical tanks—and the human heart, and it has kept the Statue of Liberty from rusting. Teflon has also been used in clothing. A man named Robert Gore noticed that the substance was not only good for coating wires, but it also could be stretched over fabric, producing what he called Gore-Tex, which breathes, letting water out but preventing it from getting in.

In an interview with the *Chicago Tribune* in 1988, Plunkett admitted he'd been lucky when Teflon was invented; the chemical reaction that led to its invention, if mishandled, could have led to an explosion! In the same interview he said, "People describe it as a lucky chance, a bit of serendipity, or a flash of brilliance. I like to think of it as a combination of all three."

Over two and a half billion pounds of Teflon have been sold over the years. Plunkett did not directly profit from his invention, because DuPont controls the rights to all substances produced by their employees, but he did receive two bonuses, one for outstanding work and another for contribution beyond the call of duty. By the time of his retirement from DuPont in 1975, he had guided development of many of their products through the manufacturing process.

On a lighter note, Teflon became so ubiquitous that U.S. Representative Pat Schroeder (D), after frying eggs for her children on a Teflon-coated pan, decided that its no-stick properties also applied to one particular politician. On August 2, 1983, on the floor of Congress, she compared then President Ronald Reagan to Teflon because, according to her, nothing wrong in his administration ever stuck to him. "Mr. Speaker," she said, "after carefully watching Ronald Reagan, he is attempting a great breakthrough in political technology; he has been perfecting the Teflon-coated presidency."

Although many at DuPont were angry at the Reagan comparison, Schroeder's phrase was quickly picked up by the popular culture and became part of the American lexicon.

Roy Plunkett was born in 1910 in New Carlisle, Ohio. He was a 1932 graduate of Manchester College in North Manchester, Indiana, and went on to receive his M.S. (1933) and Ph.D. (1936) from Ohio State University. Plunkett had a long and distinguished career at DuPont, working in several divisions. He was inducted into the Plastics Hall of Fame in 1973, the National Inventors Hall of Fame in 1985, and was honored by DuPont with an award named after him in 1988, the fiftieth anniversary of his discovery. The Plunkett Award goes to those who invent new products using Teflon.

Plunkett's lifelong association with Manchester College is reflected in the nine shelves in the Brethren Historical Library and Archives devoted to his materials, which include examples of Teflon-related items and a display that demonstrates the use of Teflon in knee joints.

# THE WINNER OF THE NOBEL PRIZE FOR PHYSICAL CHEMISTRY

**PAUL JOHN FLORY • 1910-1985**

20

*In our house we use that old saying "It's not like it's rocket science" to describe something that requires little or no mental challenge.* So one of my birthday gifts was a black t-shirt with the lettering: "Uh oh. It *Was* Rocket Science!"

Given that Brethren did not support higher education for much of their history, it's remarkable how many from earlier generations have achieved great things. It's hard to imagine any award greater than the Nobel Prize in Physical Chemistry won by Paul John Flory in 1974 for "his fundamental achievements, both theoretical and experimental, in the physical chemistry of the macromolecules" (as it says on the Nobel Prize website).

In the short autobiography for the Nobel Prize committee, Flory wrote that he was born "of Huguenot-German parentage, mine being the sixth generation native to America. My father was Ezra Flory, a clergyman-educator; my mother, nee Martha Brumbaugh, had been a schoolteacher. Both were descended from generations of farmers in the New World. They were the first of their families of record to have attended college."

Paul Flory was born in Sterling, Illinois, and was ten years old when his family moved to Elgin, where his father was the first full-time executive secretary for the General Sunday School Board. From 1920 to 1928 Ezra traveled across the denomination preaching the importance of Sunday schools, while writing for publications such as *Our Young People* and *Brethren Teacher's Monthly.*

Paul graduated from Elgin High School in 1927 and became a student at Manchester College in Indiana. Like any scientist worth his salt, he earned enough degrees to boil water, including his B.S. from Manchester College in 1931, a Ph.D. in 1934 from Ohio State, and a Sc.D. in 1950, also from Manchester. During the course of his career he worked at several large chemical and petroleum corporations; he also taught at the University of Cincinnati, Cornell University, the Mellon Institute, and Stanford University. He was a prolific writer, having produced two monographs and over three hundred scientific articles. His book, *Principles of Polymer Chemistry,* though published in 1953, remains a classic in the field, because it explains the basic concepts of, well, polymer chemistry. He is considered one of the leading scientists of the twentieth century.

Plastics, proteins, rubber, and other important compounds are made up of very complex molecules called macro-molecules. They are composed of long chains of atoms, sometimes thousands. Though these compounds are an essential part of the world in which we live, there was no satisfactory theory to explain how these molecules behaved, either theoretically or in a manufacturing sense. Dr. Flory's gift was to simplify the problem so that it could be both understood and dealt with. He introduced a new concept, theta temperature and theta point properties, to describe the place where competing forces stretch and compact these molecules, achieving an ideal state for science and industry.

True breakthroughs seem simple only in retrospect. Folks, this is rocket science to me, so the next two paragraphs, which describe his groundbreaking discoveries, come directly from Dr. Flory himself. It was 1948 when Dr. Flory held the George Fisher Baker Non-Resident Lectureship in Chemistry at Cornell University:

> It was during the Baker Lectureship that I perceived a way to treat the effect of excluded volume on the configuration of polymer chains. I had long suspected that the effect would be non-asymptotic with the length of the chain; that is, that the perturbation of the configuration by the exclusion of one segment of the chain from the space occupied by another would increase without limit as the chain is lengthened. The treatment of the effect by resort to a relatively simple "smoothed density" model confirmed this expectation and provided an expression relating the perturbation of the configuration to the chain length and the effective volume of a chain segment. It became apparent that the physical properties of dilute solutions of macromolecules could not be properly treated and comprehended without taking account of the perturbation of the macromolecule by these intramolecular interactions. The hydrodynamic theories of dilute polymer solutions developed a year or two earlier by Kirkwood and by Debye were therefore reinterpreted in

light of the excluded volume effect. Agreement with a broad range of experimental information on viscosities, diffusion coefficients and sedimentation velocities was demonstrated soon thereafter.

Out of these developments came the formulation of the hydrodynamic constant called theta, and the recognition of the Theta point at which excluded volume interactions are neutralized. Criteria for experimental identification of the Theta point are easily applied. Ideal behavior of polymers, natural and synthetic, under Theta conditions has subsequently received abundant confirmation in many laboratories. These findings are most gratifying. More importantly, they provide the essential basis for rational interpretation of physical measurements on dilute polymer solutions, and hence for the quantitative characterization of macromolecules. (Nobel Prize—"Autobiography").

Dr. Flory's work was groundbreaking, but it was not the end of his contributions to science. At the time he received the Nobel Prize, he informed the committee that two projects in particular had engaged his attention since his breakthrough. "The one concerns the spatial configuration of chain molecules and the treatment of their configuration-dependent properties by rigorous mathematical methods; the other constitutes a new approach to an old subject, namely, the thermodynamics of solutions."

The Nobel Prizes were instituted and funded by Alfred Nobel, the inventor of dynamite. Dr. Flory, in his acceptance speech, paid tribute to Nobel.

Perhaps I may be permitted to reflect briefly on Alfred Nobel. . . . Lest it seems presumptuous of me to comment on that great but little appreciated man, may I remind you that I too am a chemist. In fact, my researches have touched upon one of the principal ingredients of his epochal discoveries and inventions. I refer to nitrocellulose. To be sure, our interests in this substance differed: his of a scope leading to developments warranting world-wide fame, mine obscure by comparison. . . . I take pride in laying claim to scientific kinship to Alfred Nobel through an interest in this substance, however tenuous the connection may be.

The Nobel Prizes . . . are much better known than the man who founded them. Yet, that wise but modest man, whose extraordinary vision and perception were obscured by a self-effacing manner, would not be offended, I believe, by the contrast between his own fame in the world of 1974 and that of his prizes. He founded them from the purest of motives . . . that the prizes bear his name . . . was a decision of his executors. . . . Alfred Nobel appears to have been motivated by the conviction that science and learning should be encouraged and more widely appreciated. (Nobel Prize—"Banquet Speech")

Dr. Flory earned many other professional honors over the course of his lifetime, including the Cresson Medal of the Franklin Institute, the Priestly Medal of the American Chemical Association, and the National Medal of Science.

# THE WORLD-FAMOUS POET WHO PUT OUT FIRES

**21**

## WILLIAM STAFFORD • 1914-1993

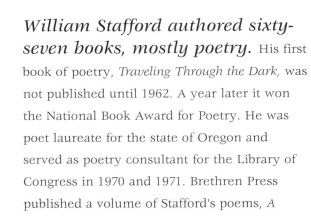

***William Stafford authored sixty-seven books, mostly poetry.*** His first book of poetry, *Traveling Through the Dark,* was not published until 1962. A year later it won the National Book Award for Poetry. He was poet laureate for the state of Oregon and served as poetry consultant for the Library of Congress in 1970 and 1971. Brethren Press published a volume of Stafford's poems, *A*

*Scripture of Leaves*, in 1989, with a new edition in 1999. The poetry is concerned with nature, the extraordinary in the commonplace of small town life, and the remembrances of the web of relationships that make us who we are.

In the latter part of his life, Stafford traveled thousands of miles each year to read his poetry and encourage other poets around the world.

But before all the fame, glory, and recognition, William Stafford endured glares, stares, and threats from his fellow Americans for taking a stand against war—not just any war, but World War II. Instead of fighting, Stafford chose to register as a conscientious objector (CO) and served his country through Civilian Public Service, supported by the three historic peace churches: the Mennonites, the Friends, and the Church of the Brethren.

For the privilege of living at the poverty level in Arkansas, Illinois, and California while working for social agencies, building and maintaining roads and trails, and fighting forest fires, Stafford was paid $2.50 a month—by the Church of the Brethren.

The genteel poverty of service is a thread that runs throughout Stafford's book *Down in My Heart*, written as the thesis for his master's degree from the University of Kansas in 1945 and published by Brethren Press in 1947. He addresses his story to a fellow CO, whom he calls "George," who lies unconscious in a prison hospital bed. (Stafford warns that he has changed the names because their stand was no more popular after the war than it was during the conflict.) When the war ended George felt he had not protested enough, went AWOL, was sentenced to prison, and eventually went on a hunger strike.

The book opens with Stafford's description of a near-riot that developed when he and a few others were enjoying the sun "near the depot one Sunday afternoon in McNeil, Arkansas, and talked cordially with some of the men who were loafing around in the Sabbath calm."

One of their party is painting a watercolor, another writing a poem, and Stafford himself is reading "Leaves of Grass" by Walt Whitman. Once it becomes known that the group consists of COs, the day turns dangerous. Only the timely arrival of a police officer keeps the situation under control. Later, a preacher who visits them begs them not to look down on the locals as "hicks because they see you as spies and dangerous men." He reminds the COs that the government has spent millions instilling an attitude of suspicion.

It's not the last time they face personal danger, but the book is more about reconciliation and the possibility of transformation. While working in the wilderness with an arrogant and abusive overseer, the COs protest the use of racial slurs and threats of violence by simply ceasing to cooperate, regardless of the possible consequences. Through dialogue and negotiation they defuse a tense situation as respect develops between former adversaries.

There's a CO wedding, a week spent on furlough with a philosopher, a battle with a fire that brings with it an opportunity for better food, and finally the very odd day when the war ends and Stafford wonders, with the others, how can they celebrate? The sense of alienation, of being a stranger in a strange land, runs throughout the piece, perhaps nowhere more than in the chapter on victory in Japan.

> Soon they will resume their interrupted lives, but the question of whether they have really made a difference, and if they can resume their old lives with integrity if it means having benefitted from a new and terrible atomic weapon, haunts them.

That final question—Was it all worth it?—is one that many CPSers struggled with. Though many books have been written about the experiences of conscientious objectors, *Down in My Heart* is important because it was written in a stark and simple prose that somehow manages to be poetry, by a poet long before he became known as a famous poet. "We watched the celebration till dark," he writes, "and then . . . we waded through the confetti back to the camp truck, and left the celebrating city to go back to our island of a camp—more foreigners than ever."

*Down in My Heart* was reprinted by Brethren Press in 1971 during the Vietnam conflict so that (according to the book jacket) "a new generation whose sense of social responsibility leads them to stand fast against conscription and violence . . . may find out how it felt to say NO back then."

William Stafford was born in 1914 in Hutchinson, Kansas. He earned his bachelor's degree from the University of Kansas in 1937, but before then he'd worked in sugar beet fields, on construction sites, and at oil refineries. In 1944 he married Dorothy Hope Frantz. They were the parents of four children. After the war he was a high school teacher and worked as the secretary to the director of Church World Service while completing work on his master's degree at the University of Kansas in 1945.

# THE RASPBERRY SEED UNDER THE PRESIDENT'S DENTURES

## 22

**PAUL HUME • 1915-2001**

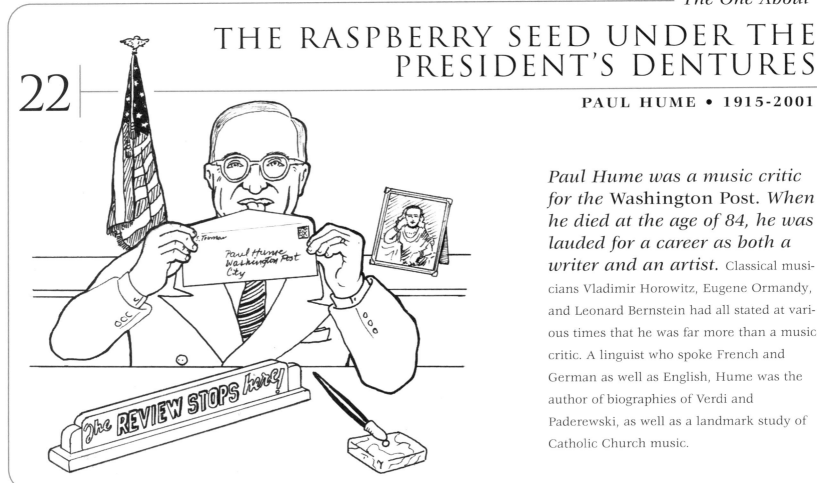

*Paul Hume was a music critic for the* Washington Post. *When he died at the age of 84, he was lauded for a career as both a writer and an artist.* Classical musicians Vladimir Horowitz, Eugene Ormandy, and Leonard Bernstein had all stated at various times that he was far more than a music critic. A linguist who spoke French and German as well as English, Hume was the author of biographies of Verdi and Paderewski, as well as a landmark study of Catholic Church music.

He was an accomplished musician who sang baritone solos and performed organ recitals at the Washington National Cathedral in the 1950s, directed the Georgetown University Glee Club, and was the organizer of a choir of madrigal singers. He won a Peabody Award for broadcasting, was awarded numerous honorary doctorates, and hosted programs on a classical music station in Washington, D.C.

Paul Hume was a man of principle, serving as a conscientious objector during World War II, which provides his connection to the Brethren. He was originally assigned to a Civilian Public Service camp, but in 1942 he was transferred to the headquarters of the National Service Board in Washington.

He was a man of many talents, but he will always be known for one incident, a famous review he wrote.

It was 1950, the height of the Cold War. The Red Scare was in full force, the Korean War was going badly, and Charlie Ross, the best friend of President Harry Truman, had just died unexpectedly.

Nevertheless, the president's daughter, Margaret, whose talent as a singer was debatable, was scheduled to sing before a sellout crowd of 3,500 at Constitution Hall. Though Margaret had been taking singing lessons for many years and giving concerts, her friend and opera star, Helen Traubel, is said to have suggested that she not rush into performing until she had more training. That night the concert went forward but Truman insisted that no one tell his daughter about Ross.

Margaret Truman sang "a light program" and was called back for four encores. Truman, a self-acclaimed musicologist and accomplished pianist, loved Margaret's performance despite his sadness over the loss of his friend. There was a complimentary review in the Washington *Times-Herald,* and many others congratulated her after the performance.

Margaret herself remembers, "I was the only one in Constitution Hall who did not know about [Ross's death]. . . . Charlie's death may have made many people in the audience feel that it was bad taste for me to be singing at all. At any rate, I soon sensed there was something wrong with their reaction. At the time I blamed it on Korea. I was sure it had nothing to do with the music. In fact, I thought it was one of my better performances. At intermission, the music critic for the *Times-Herald* came backstage and congratulated me."

But the opinion was not unanimous. The next morning President Truman opened his *Post* at 5:30 a.m., and read Paul Hume's review, which read, in part:

> Miss Truman is a unique American phenomenon with a pleasant voice of little size and fair quality. She is extremely attractive on stage. . . . Yet Miss Truman cannot sing very well. She is flat a good deal of the time—more last night than at any time we have heard her in past years. There are few moments during her recital when one can relax and feel confident that she will make her goal, which is the end of the song.
>
> Miss Truman has not improved in the years we have heard her . . . she still cannot sing with anything approaching professional finish.
>
> She communicates almost nothing of the music she presents. . . . And still the public goes and pays the same price it would for the world's finest singers. . . . It is an extremely unpleasant duty to record such unhappy facts about so honestly appealing a person. But as long as Truman sings as she has for three years, and does today, we seem to have no recourse unless it is to omit comment on her programs altogether. (McCullough 827-828)

As Margaret remembers, Truman exploded:

> Dad saw red. For him, *this* was the last straw. His best friend had just died, the world situation was going from bad to awful, and now a critic was attacking his daughter with what seemed more malice than judgment. (Truman 502)

President Truman was used to writing vitriolic letters expressing his feelings, often in colorful language, but generally he changed his mind about mailing such letters. Many times his friend Charlie Ross would talk him out of sending the worst of these. But Ross was gone, and after penning the note in haste, Truman walked over to the White House and found a messenger willing to drop it off in the post office. By the time his advisors learned of what he'd done, it was too late. He had written:

> Mr. Hume: I've just read your lousy review of Margaret's concert. I've come to the conclusion that you are an "eight ulcer man on four ulcer pay."
>
> It seems to me that you are a frustrated old man [*Hume was thirty-four*] who wishes he could have been successful. When you write such poppy-cock as was in the back section of the paper you work for, it shows conclusively that you're off the beam and at least four of your ulcers are at work.
>
> Some day I hope to meet you. When that happens you'll need a new nose, a lot of beefsteak for black eyes, and perhaps a supporter below!
>
> [Westbrook] Pegler, a gutter snipe, is a gentleman alongside you. I hope you'll accept that statement as a worse insult than a reflection on your ancestry. (McCullough 829)

Now Hume was not a frustrated old man or a Pegler either. (Westbrook Pegler was a yellow journalist of the worst sort.) When Truman's letter was made public, Truman's staff worried about the effect it would have on his presidency.

On December 9, 1950, Truman wrote in his diary:

Margie held a concert here in D.C. on Dec. 5th. It was a good one. She was well accompanied by a young pianist by the name of Allison, whose father is a Baptist preacher in Augusta, Georgia. Young Allison played two pieces after the intermission, one of which was the great A flat Chopin Waltz Opus 42. He did it as well as it could be done and I've heard Paderewski, Moritz Rosenthal, and Joseph Lhevinne play it.

A frustrated critic on the *Washington Post* wrote a lousy review. The only thing, General Marshall said, he didn't criticize was the varnish on the piano. He put my "baby" as low as he could and he made the young accompanist look like a dub.

It upset me, and I wrote him what I thought of him. I told him he is lower than Pegler and that was intended to be an insult worse than a reflection on his ancestry. I would never reflect on a man's mother because mothers are not to be attacked although mine has [been]!

Well, I've had a grand time this day. I've been accused of putting my "baby" who is the "apple of my eye" in a bad position. I don't think that is so. She doesn't either—thank the Almighty. (Ferrell)

In her book about her father, Margaret wrote:

Dad discussed the letter with his aides and was annoyed to find that they all thought it was a mistake. They felt that it damaged his image as President and would only add to his political difficulties. "Wait till the mail comes in," Dad said, "I'll make you a bet that eighty percent of it is on my side of the argument."

A week later, after a staff meeting, Dad ordered everybody to follow him, and they marched to the mail room. The clerks had stacked the thousands of "Hume" letters received in piles and made up a chart showing the percentages for and against the President. Slightly over 80 percent favored Dad's defense of me. Most of the letter writers were mothers who said they understood exactly how Dad felt and would have expected their husbands to defend their daughters the same way. (503)

But most writers have noted that the letters indicated that public opinion ran against the president two to one. Hume himself told reporters that he sympathized with the president. He was quoted as saying, "I can only say that a man suffering the loss of a friend and carrying the burden of the present world crisis ought to be indulged in an occasional outburst of temper" (McCullough 830). And some months later, when controversy swirled around the president's firing of the popular General Douglas MacArthur, Hume wrote a letter of support.

Some newspapers even questioned President Truman's stability and mental competence, and the controversy remained one of the most remembered incidents of his presidency.

Years later Paul Hume traveled to Kansas City to review a concert and drove out to Truman's library, where the former president spent much of his time. They had what Hume called a "wonderful visit." Apparently the president's wife, Bess, was skeptical about the report of the meeting, but she was convinced when they found themselves sitting across the aisle from each other at the concert that night and Truman said, "See, I told you that Paul Hume was in my office today" (McCullough 976).

# THE BROTHER WHO SAVED US FROM THE MARTIANS

## 23

OTIS "SLIM" WHITMAN • 1924-

PAAF!

*There we were—the whole planet absolutely powerless— falling into the grip of the malevolent Martians, who were destroying us one by one as well as wholesale.* That's when the hero's grandmother (who's a little hard of hearing and doesn't notice this particularly evil-looking Martian sneaking up behind her in the nursing home, about to blow her away) puts on one of her Slim Whitman records and the Martian's head explodes.

And then *all* the Martians explode! The hero rigs up his truck to play the music, sending the Slim Whitman song "Indian Love Call" out over the airwaves. Word gets around and soon everyone is playing his music all over the world until the heads of all the Martians everywhere blow up and their ships fall into the sea and a mariachi band plays "The Star-Spangled Banner" on the steps of the White House ruins while the president's daughter (she's the only member of the family left alive) gives the hero a medal, and he suggests we all try living in teepees. And that's not even telling about the part where Tom Jones sings "It's Not Unusual."

Okay, this didn't really happen, but it's all part of the movie *Mars Attacks!* and, since Slim Whitman is a member of the Church of the Brethren, he is the one who saves the world.

Whew!

Back to reality. Slim Whitman is one of the most popular singers in England and on the Continent, but he may be better known in the United States for the part his song played in the movie *Mars Attacks!* than for his singing career. Still, over the years he has earned the title of "America's Foremost Folksinger." He had his first No. 1 hit in the United Kingdom in 1955 with "Rose Marie." By staying in the top spot for eleven weeks, it set a record that lasted thirty-six years. This success overseas led to an invitation to join the Grand Ole Opry in 1957 along with an appearance in the film *Jamboree*.

Otis Dewey Whitman, Jr., was born in 1924 in Tampa, Florida. The singer/songwriter is a self-taught, left-handed guitarist, even though he is a natural right-hander, because he lost most of the second finger on his left hand in an accident. After serving in the Navy during World War II, Whitman worked at a Tampa shipyard, but also performed with a band called the Variety Rhythm Boys. Even after he was discovered by Colonel Tom Parker (who would later become Elvis Presley's manager), released his first single (in 1948), went on tour, and became a regular on radio, it was still necessary for him to keep a part-time job.

Within a few years, however, with the release of songs like "Love Song of the Waterfall" and "Indian Love Call," Whitman finally made enough of a mark that he could perform and record full time. He struck a chord by avoiding the "world done him wrong" sort of song and instead concentrated on romantic ballads about love and the simple joys of life.

His career was fairly productive and he enjoyed a good deal of success, but in 1974 he called an end to new recording, figuring things had run their course. Surprisingly, though, when he filmed a commercial in 1979 to coincide with a greatest-hits release compiled by Suffolk Marketing, things took off again. *All My Best* sold more records than any other album marketed on television. He followed that a year later with *Just For You* in 1980, *Best Loved Favorites* in 1989, and *20 Precious Memories* in 1991. He toured extensively in Europe and Australia. And as recently as 2002 he set out on a tour of the British Isles, where he remains just as popular as ever.

In the midst of that second career, Brethren Press published Whitman's biography, titled *Mr. Songman.* The book, written by Ken Gibble, was published by Brethren Press in 1982 because, well, Slim Whitman is Brethren. He is an active member of the Jacksonville (Fla.) Church of the Brethren and has appeared at the Church of the Brethren Annual Conference.

It is clear from Gibble's book that Whitman is genuinely humble and genuinely loved. In Europe and England he is appreciated for his honesty, for the way he goes out of his way to please his fans, and the fact that he always puts his church and his family first. Slim has never presented himself as a perfect saint, but his choices—to avoid songs about drinking, cheating on a marriage, or deliberately living beyond the bounds of the Christian faith—have served him well in the long run.

His story is one of classic underpromotion, and yet he has triumphed despite that. He is genuine and that seems to count for something.

Several times in his career his unique vocal style has led to a great deal of kidding, and on occasion some have promoted concerts or featured him in movies, such as *Mars Attacks!*, to mock him. These efforts inevitably have led to new fans who, once they get used to his unique styling, realize that there is no one quite like him.

Whitman once said the key to his success is that no one else was singing "Red River Valley" at the time and he was, but there is obviously more than that. Again and again, when his career seemed over—a fact that never overly distressed him—he has risen again to the forefront not by remolding himself, but by sticking with the songs he authentically loves.

It is clear that Slim's audiences see him as one of themselves—an honest, church-going, self-effacing, level-headed, blue-collar, down-home kind of fellow—and it's not an act.

It's easy to find out if this is all true. Take the Slim Whitman test. Buy, borrow, download, and otherwise obtain (legally) one of his albums and play it. It's great to be able to say that he's one of us.

# THE VAULTING VICAR WHO MUST HAVE HAD HIS WHEATIES

## 24

### BOB RICHARDS • 1926-

*The commercial was an icon in the early days of television: the healthy, clean-cut athlete, every inch the perfect physical specimen, looking directly into the camera and reminding us* that Wheaties is "The Breakfast of Champions." It was also a tough sell. In an era of sugar-sweet cereals and a general lack of knowledge about nutrition, the pitchman was trying to convince the children of America to eat something healthful and good for them, rather than something tasty.

But that was no ordinary athlete asking us to do the right thing. It was Bob Richards, known variously as the Vaulting Vicar, the Decathlon Deacon, the Flying Parson, and the Pole-Vaulting Parson, and at the time both a member and minister in the Church of the Brethren.

Bob Richards was the only person to win two vaulting gold medals and three medals of any color in the pole vault at the Olympic Games, competing in 1948, 1952, and 1956. In an era when amateur athletes outside the Iron Curtain really had to remain amateurs, Richards supported his family and his sports career by supplementing his salary as a professor at La Verne College and giving as many as three hundred speeches and sermons a year.

Magazine articles about Richards emphasize his former reputation as a young tough before he found the Lord, that he was part of a gang in Champaign, Illinois, most of whose members went to prison. In later years Richards tried to soften the legend just a bit, making it clear, in his opinion, that they were troublemakers but hardly the hard-core criminals as they were portrayed. He admitted he was constantly in fights, but "there was no criminality. . . . Sometimes we'd steal fruit, and things like that."

What Richards did emphasize in every account over the years was the part played by Merlin Garber, the pastor of the local Church of the Brethren. When Richards was sixteen, he was rebuffed by a girl because he did not have a church life, so he went to worship at the church he had walked by many times over the years and was welcomed by Garber, despite his lack of proper dress or understanding of church ways. Garber nurtured the teenager, encouraging him and for a time taking him into his home. Garber was a factor in Richards' choosing to attend Bridgewater College in Virginia.

Richards was always athletic. According to the story, he could do thirty chin-ups at the age of eight, was active in city and YMCA athletics, and was willing to try anything in junior high and high school, wrestling the first time, for instance, as an emergency substitute and winning his first match without ever having practiced.

He became a pole-vaulter in a similar fashion. He was only twelve years old when his track coach asked him to fill a gap when there was no one else to compete in that event. He won the event.

Richards did not concentrate solely on the pole vault until he was twenty. Although he was shorter than what was considered the ideal height in those days (he was only five-foot ten), Richards became only the second person to exceed fifteen feet in the era before modern poles made greater heights possible.

While at Bridgewater College, Richards played basketball and would regularly win six events at every track meet: the pole vault, high and low hurdles, broad and high jumps, and the javelin. As he matured between his first and second year, he lost his reputation as a hothead.

By the end of the second year in college, Richards had married Mary Leah Cline of Vienna, Virginia, who was also the niece of the college president. In order to be able to afford marriage and college, he and his wife moved back to Illinois to live with the Garbers while attending the University of Illinois in Champaign. He later attended Bethany Theological Seminary.

In an era when western athletes were expected to remain strict amateurs, without any support from their own countries and Olympic committees, and Communist competitors were virtual professionals supported by their governments, Richards won a bronze in his event at the 1948 London Olympics. In 1951 he won the Sullivan Award as outstanding amateur athlete. Richards won a gold medal in 1952 at Helsinki and again in 1956 in Melbourne, where he also competed in the decathlon.

In the meantime Richards was licensed and then ordained by the Church of the Brethren. He would teach three religion courses in the fall semester at La Verne College in California, then spend the spring semester lecturing and preaching on behalf of the college while training and attending meets. He often practiced indoors in the college gymnasium, vaulting onto an elevated stage.

All along the way he would emphasize the importance of his faith to his success. "I can sincerely say I owe my athletic achievements to the power of the Lord," he said on more than one occasion.

Following his final Olympics, Richards "went professional." He was not paid for competing as an athlete, but he was reimbursed for his reputation, which rendered him ineligible for further amateur competition. The most visible of these endorsements was with Wheaties, known since the 1930s as the Breakfast of Champions for its association with the character "Jack Armstrong, All-American Boy." In the past some athletes had appeared on other parts of the box, but Richards was the first to be depicted on the front in 1958. He appeared in television commercials and headed the Wheaties Sports Federation, making motivational speeches, how-to films, and writing books and manuals.

Over the years Richards emphasized that he never prayed to win, only for strength to be able to compete. Years later, in an interview with *La Verne Magazine*, he contested the popular view of winning and specifically the oft-quoted statement by the late Vince Lombardi that winning isn't everything, it's the only thing. "He was wrong," Richards said. "Being No. 2 is just as good as being No. 1. It is in the participating, in being in the arena, that makes winners in life. It's having a dream that makes the difference."

Evidently the Pole-Vaulting Parson practiced what he preached. A *New York Times* article, describing his second Olympic gold medal, returns time and again to the theme of the international competitors, especially Richards, encouraging each other to fly higher and higher and consoling each other when failing.

Richards has been honored many times in many ways. Over the years he has dropped his association with the ministry and with the Church of the Brethren. He admits that his heavy speaking schedule cost him his first marriage; he is currently active in breeding miniature horses in partnership with his second wife. (A complete list of his honors can be found at < http://www.olympianranch.com/about.html >.

In an interview with *La Verne Magazine* staff in the early nineties, Richards descried the waste of war. "We slaughtered two million people in Vietnam. In Desert Storm alone we slaughtered 150,000 people, and the American people are waving flags and saying what a great thing it was. It was *horrible.* But that's what wins elections. It is this type of thing that makes Bush popular. What a primitive system. War, killing, and slaughter!" He concluded by saying, "It seems to me that the ultimate goal or aim in society should be to help each other, not kill each other off. We should be feeding five million people; two-thirds of the world's population is hungry. Can you imagine how many of those people are starving children?"

# THE ACTOR WITH PRINCIPLES

**DON MURRAY • 1929-**

## 25

*When Don Murray returned from the service in 1956, he discovered that his agent had arranged far more television and film projects than he could imagine.* Soon he would be acting with the likes of Marilyn Monroe, Hope Lange, Helen Hayes, and Mary Martin. It was quite a step for someone who had been the classic struggling actor, depending on the kindness of friends and family to make ends meet.

His service, you see, had not been with a branch of the armed forces. Don Murray had taken the unconventional step of following his conscience, fighting a long legal battle to be classified as a conscientious objector, and signing on with the Brethren Service Commission to serve in Europe aiding refugees.

Don Murray grew up in a show business family. His father, a Roman Catholic, managed shows on Broadway, and his mother was a former Ziegfeld Follies girl and sang with the choir at her Congregational church. Though he was high spirited by nature and often in trouble, Don experienced church and Sunday school as a regular part of family life.

Murray's sense of social justice was sparked at the multi-racial Congregational church camps, held at Blairstown, New Jersey. He found that he was opposed to war and had thought through his position by the time he registered for the draft at the age of eighteen. Though his mother, father, and older brother (who had served as a Marine during World War II) did not agree with his position, they respected it because they knew it was his sincere belief. Don experienced taunting from his colleagues in the theater, but by the time he was called before the draft board and threatened with prosecution and imprisonment, he had their support as he stood up to the courts. He was investigated by the FBI for two years and questioned by both his local draft board and by officials in Washington, D.C. At one point, as his status was reviewed by a judge, his mother came forward to say, "I have one son who was a Marine and another who is a conscientious objector. I am equally proud of them both."

Murray himself, in an interview, remembered how he had to fight the prejudice of the United States attorney in charge of the case. The attorney, whose brother was a priest, automatically rejected the claims of any Catholic to being a conscientious objector."

Murray added, "In my case . . . he took the position that show business was a business with very loose morals, and my convictions were not serious, that I was trying to avoid going into the service because I had a successful Broadway career going and I wanted to take advantage of lucrative film offers. The fact was, as I pointed out, I had some offers and I turned them all down. There were no film offers because I said no to all of them. He asked me why and I said I didn't believe they were worthy films." That seemed to surprise the attorney who, according to Murray, answered with surprise, "You mean to tell me that actors have moral convictions?"

In a private interview, the U.S. Attorney asked him to name the Ten Commandments. "And I could only name nine. Shame on me. I got all the obscure ones, and I forgot the obvious one, which was adultery!" The attorney saw this as one more sign of an actor's immorality. Murray was finally classified as a CO at the age of twenty-two, and after being rejected for alternative service by the Red Cross, American Field Service, and the Korean Reconstruction Agency, he was accepted by the Brethren.

Murray canceled auditions for three Broadway plays and one television play and was soon in New Windsor, Maryland, training for work overseas. He knew nothing about the Brethren: "I had expected to find little men wearing beards. Instead I found a happy group of people who were really putting their religion into action. Suddenly I felt as if my whole life had pointed to this purpose. My bed was a foot too short, but I slept like a rock that night."

In March 1953, three months later, he sailed for Europe and was posted in Kassel, Germany, where he worked as a bricklayer, repairing a city that still lay in ruins from the war. He became actively involved in the community and with youth activities in the area, learning German as he went along. And he was also baptized Brethren in the Fulda River in the middle of winter. After a year Murray received a letter from the Congregational Church asking him to direct a relief center for refugees in Naples, Italy. He was shocked by what he saw. There were fifty thousand impoverished refugees of all ages living in slums behind barbed wire. Many of the children had tuberculosis. Most lived on one meal a day. Soon he was learning Italian and distributing food and clothing. Many of the younger ones had turned to street crime to better their lives.

Confronted by the fact that the people had no hope, Don started a Boys Club, worked with refugees to create a crafts program, and found a market for their crafts by creating bazaars on American military bases. Soon he was making a difference.

He was also killing himself. He contracted hepatitis, lost thirty pounds, developed pneumonia and nearly died, especially when he returned to work too soon.

In the midst of all this, he found time for his creative work and developed a Christmas nativity program that he attempted to present on Christmas Eve 1954, before 1,200 refugees at a camp near Capua, Italy. "It was a defining moment," Murray said in our interview. He recalled the skepticism of those in charge of the camps, and the obstacles they put up, forcing him to change the venue; the camp director told him it was a useless activity, that the only thing the refugees cared about was food, sleep, and drinking. But for Murray it was part of the education process to help the refugees develop a sense of hope and self-worth. "We went on a lot of junkets with the class. I took them to all these historical places. They would have lectures about what they were seeing." Since they were also learning English, the pageant would be in English.

But there were more obstacles on the day of the program. Normally Murray would take two streetcars and three buses to get to the camp, requiring as much as two hours travel time. But for the special event, "I was supposed to get a car that night. I had all the decorations with me, big boxes." But there was a mistake and no car. Forced to take public transit and struggling with all his equipment, he arrived very late. "I thought . . . it was going to be a disaster. I found that the refugees themselves had taken the initiative and made some makeshift decorations and it was all decorated."

The bitterness of the refugees spilled over as the music was drowned out by jeers and objects were thrown on the stage.

In broken Italian Don reminded the people, "We are gathered here tonight from different national origins and of different religious beliefs—Christians, Moslems, Jews and many others. But one thing we can all share—if not a worship of Jesus

Christ as divine, then a great respect for him as a man. It is to honor that respect that we present this program." By the time the program was finished, the audience demanded it be presented again.

Murray stayed six months beyond his two-year enlistment, earning the standard $7.50 a month.

Those who knew Don Murray felt that his experiences had deepened his talents as an actor, and it wasn't long before he was starring on stage and screen. His films included *Bus Stop* (for which he received an Academy Award nomination), *Hatful of Rain*, and *Bachelor Party*. Looking back on his service work, Murray said, "That was probably the major contribution that I will have made. Of course Ken [Kreider] was a big part of that, the Brethren were a big part of that, and the Congregational Christian Social Workers were a part of that." The combination of different groups working together was crucial, in his mind.

Murray's service in Europe had opened his eyes to the suffering of innocent refugees in Europe, and he resolved to do something about it. His return to sudden fame—and more income—in the late fifties and early sixties enabled him to give a little HELP (Homeless European Land Program), as he called the program he founded to help European refugees who were still behind barbed wire years after fleeing the ravages of Nazism and Communism. The organization purchased land and resettled refugees on farms. Ultimately, after some fits and starts, refugee families began to experience a sense of ownership and pride. J. Kenneth Kreider, in his book *A Cup of Cold Water,* (and who himself played a major role in maintaining and operating the program on the ground in Europe) wrote: "After nearly ten years of successful operation, the cooperative was dissolved in 1966 and divided among the refugees who had established permanent residence. . . . Don Murray's dream had become reality. He had made it possible for victims of World War II to help make a new start in life" (311). In his work Murray emphasized the importance of making a difference, and articles that appeared in both religious and popular periodicals emphasized his membership in the Church of the Brethren and his relief work.

Don went on to write and produce films that he felt reflected his principles, such as *Sweet Love, Bitter, Hoodlum Priest,* and *The Cross and the Switchblade. Hoodlum Priest* was based on the real life story of a death row chaplain and had a strong anti-death penalty theme.

Over the years he continued to work actively in television and movies. One of his best known parts was the role of Sid Fairgate on the popular TV show *Knot's Landing,* derisively referred to as "Saint Sid" by the other characters for his moral principles.

Murray has continued to appear in television and films to this day. He has sixty-four major credits in film and television roles, according to one filmography, and remains actively involved in film projects.

Murray also played a crucial but largely untold role (at least until the publication of *A Cup of Cold Water*) in bringing Brethren Volunteer Service to the attention of those in power as a model for the Peace Corps. He laughed as he recalled having a small role in the 1952 presidential campaign because he had no so-called celebrity. But after starring in the film *Bus Stop,* he was asked by the Democratic National Committee prior to the 1956 presidential election "to go to Hibbing [Minnesota] to introduce [vice presidential candidate C. Estes] Kefauver." Again and again he practiced his speech, which, in his own words, was simply, "Ladies and Gentlemen the next vice president, C. Estes Kefauver." Murray remembered, "That's all I was prepared to do, that one sentence. I was on the podium. Two of the greatest orators were to speak. One was Victor Reuther, of the AFL-CIO, the other was Hubert Humphrey. They gave fabulous speeches. As Humphrey was finishing up and Kefauver was supposed to come on next, the guy that organized [the event] whispered that Sen. Kefauver's plane is late and we need you to stall for time and we need you to make a speech. *What about?* Hollywood. That's what they want to hear from you anyway. *How long?* We'll let you know. They introduced me and I mouthed in a loud stage whisper. *How long?* Half an hour. . . .

"Instead of telling Hollywood stories (they were boring and I didn't know enough anyway), I started to talk about Brethren Service. They became very enthralled, and, as a matter of fact, right before I summed up what I was going to say, Senator Kefauver appeared in the doorway, eight thousand people there, I could see him. I kept him waiting a couple of minutes because I wanted to finish up my point."

Apparently his impromptu speech did not go unnoticed. According to Murray, Senator Hubert Humphrey took a personal interest in the "peace corps" idea and thought he had convinced President Eisenhower to institute such a program for the United States, but in the end other presidential advisors convinced him that modern youth did not have enough enthusiasm and idealism to make the program work and that it would be a black mark on his administration. The next administration, however, did not share those convictions, and Humphrey was able to convince President Kennedy, who instituted the Peace Corps.

Murray considers his relationship to the Brethren today as very warm. There are no Brethren congregations in Santa Barbara, where he lives, but he has kept in touch with the Brethren he knew well during his Brethren Service days. He recalled visiting Dale Aukerman in New Windsor before his death. And with first-place winnings from the celebrity portion of the Crosby golf tournament, he was able to fund a year-long trip and transportation for Dale's son, Daniel, a doctor who was raising money to work in Africa.

# THE RESURRECTION OF THE UNFORGETTABLE VOICE

**26**

**JAMES EARL JONES • 1931-**

*The voice is instantly recognizable—familiar to millions around the world as the voice of Darth Vader* in the *Star Wars* saga; in his role as Alex Haley in the groundbreaking miniseries *Roots* (1979); and as the voice of CNN, the world's first twenty-four-hour news station. James Earl Jones is one of the best-known actors in the world, with an unforgettable voice. He makes an impression even when he is not visible. On stage, screen, television, and radio, the rich, deep, timbre of his voice bespeaks stability, nobility, and truth.

But it's a little known fact that the world might never have heard this voice were it not for the encouragement of a Brethren teacher in a little town with the unlikely name of Brethren, Michigan.

Donald Crouch, a former college professor and an ordained minister in the Church of the Brethren, had retired to Michigan. But he came out of retirement when he discovered that the local high school did not have a qualified literature and Latin instructor. It was in the 1930s that a young boy named James Earl Jones moved with his grandparents from Mississippi to rural Michigan, first attending elementary school and then Norman Dickson High School in Brethren.

Daunted by a strange environment in which he was one of a very few African Americans in a white population, Jones struggled with a speech impediment, battling a debilitating stutter that rendered him virtually silent. That is, until he met Donald Crouch.

"He dropped his plow and came back as a teacher, lucky for us," Jones said in a *Messenger* interview. Crouch instilled in his pupils a love for "good literature—Shakespeare, Emerson, Longfellow," Jones noted in his autobiography. These were authors who were to inspire him in his own life.

During that time government shipments of staples and perishables would arrive by train in Brethren, including Florida grapefruit. "The taste of it knocked me out, the pure, juicy luxury of grapefruit in winter," Jones remembered. "I decided to write a poem about it, patterned after the poem I knew best—Longfellow's 'Song of Hiawatha.' "

When Crouch discovered that his silent student was a poet, he challenged Jones to read it aloud, suggesting that it was one way to prove that it was his own creation and not a something he had copied from elsewhere.

According to Jones, "My honor was at stake. Plagiarism was bad business. I had written every word of this poem myself. I would never copy someone else's poem and claim it for my own."

Despite the trauma of opening his mouth in front of the class, Jones rose to the challenge.

"I opened my mouth—and to my astonishment, the words flowed out smoothly, every one of them. There was no stutter. All of us were amazed not so much by the poem as by the performance.

"Professor Crouch and I had stumbled on a principle that speech therapists and psychologists understand. The written word is safe for the stutterer. The script is a sanctuary. I could read from the paper the words I had composed there, and speak as fluently as anybody in the class."

As a result of that epiphany, Jones began to recite the classics and went on to pursue drama and debate.

After one forensics meet in Traverse City, Jones recalled that the prize he won was diminished by another experience he and Crouch shared afterwards. "We went to lunch at a fine restaurant in Traverse City. I had never been to such a nice place.

" 'No colored people will be served here,' a voice told us.

"Somehow that arbitrary wall always took me by surprise. We left. I do not remember what we did after that."

Crouch continued to encourage Jones even after he graduated from high school and went on to the University of Michigan. At one point he gave him the advice to read Emerson, but to "speak poetry."

Crouch remained for James Earl Jones his most influential teacher. "What impressed me most about him was his broad thinking. He wanted to open our minds up to the larger world. . . . Especially during election times. He would really make us think and not get caught into what was handed down to us blindly from our families and our class or our social peers."

The two men remained lifelong friends until Crouch's death in 1982. Jones went on to star in Broadway plays, more than two hundred movies, and many commercials. He received the Kennedy Center Honor for lifetime achievement in the performing arts in December 2002.

# THE COUPLE WHO TOOK THE BRETHREN PATH TO FAME AND INFLUENCE

**ANDREW YOUNG • 1932-   AND   JEAN CHILDS YOUNG • 1933-1994**

## 27

*In a 2006 radio interview, Andrew Young recalled, "I was fortunate enough to marry a wife who had grown up in the Church of the Brethren tradition,* a devout pacifist position, and went to school in Manchester College in Indiana."

Both Andrew Young and his wife, Jean Childs Young, experienced difficult childhoods combating the racism endemic in the South.

Both went on to accomplish great things—and both can point to the Church of the Brethren as an important influence in their choice to work for civil rights in a nonviolent fashion.

Andrew Young was a top aide to Martin Luther King, Jr., during the civil rights movement. He served three terms in the U.S. House of Representatives from the Fifth Congressional District of Georgia, and in 1977, appointed by President Jimmy Carter, he became the first African-American ambassador to the United Nations. Young served two terms as mayor of Atlanta and was co-chairman of the Centennial Olympic Games in 1996. He has been president of the National Council of Churches, is a published author, and has received many national and international awards.

Young is now chairman of Good Works International and a professor of public policy at the Andrew Young School of Policy Studies at Georgia State University. He is an ordained minister with the United Church of Christ and a human rights activist.

Jean Childs Young was a singular person in her own right. She was born in Marion, Alabama, also the home of Coretta Scott (King). She excelled in athletics her whole life and was a teacher, an advocate for children's right, and a consultant, lecturer, and organizer. Although it was her husband who often made headlines, she too accomplished many things in her life. In 1980 she was the chair of the U.S. Commission on the International Year of the Child, a program of the United Nations. She established the Atlanta Task Force on Education and served as its chair for seven terms. She was co-founder of the Atlanta-Fulton Commission on Children and Youth.

For both Andrew and Jean, their connection with the Brethren provided a profound influence on their lives. Jean Childs Young attended Manchester College in North Manchester, Indiana. Andrew Young was a leader at Camp Mack in Indiana. Both went to the same Brethren Service Commission workcamp in Europe in 1953, helping to build refugee camps for those fleeing Communism.

In a speech at Camp Mack in the year 2000, Andrew Young recalled how his path came to intersect the Church of the Brethren: "Something happened at Camp Mack that moved me in the right direction. Camp Mack was the highlight of my first summer after graduating from Howard University." Confused about his life's direction, he told his father that he had decided not to pursue a career as a dentist. As that summer in 1951 began, he first went with his family to King's Mountain in South Carolina.

"I went out for a run," he recalled. "I literally ran to the top of the mountain. Out of breath, looking out at the universe, I decided that everything had a purpose, and that there was a purpose for me too."

Then he attended an integrated camp in Texas where he met many Christians, and, as a result of that week in camp, he was asked to work as a volunteer for a week at Camp Mack in Milford, Indiana.

In a speech given at Camp Mack, Young reflected on that experience: "I got here and lived here in one of these cabins." Referring to the children's book *Cornfields That Will Grow People,* a history of Camp Mack, he remembered, "I was one of those people grown in this cornfield. That was forty-nine years ago. I don't remember much here besides the corn." But he recalled a great roaring fireplace, as well as what he called laughingly a strange custom of people taking turns at rubbing each other's backs.

More important, he said, "I was given a little book by Don Bowman called *Nehru on Gandhi.* It was my introduction to nonviolence. I was a child of World War II. I remember Roosevelt saying the only thing we have to fear is fear itself. The only things I read were war stories and sport stories. This was a revolutionary notion, that you could change the world without violence. Don didn't preach about it. He just handed me the book."

While at Camp Mack, Young met another black camper from Mozambique who said he would make it his life's work to change Africa. Young decided he wanted to change the South.

"I had grown up among the Ku Klux Klan," he said. "Though I didn't know it at the time, that week set the direction for my ministry. I became a part of Martin Luther King's nonviolent movement.

Seminary education followed. Along the way he met Jean Childs.

He followed her to Europe as part of Brethren Volunteer Service. Andrew Young remembered in a radio interview, "Jean . . . [and] I went to an ecumenical work camp. The Church of the Brethren, after the war [founded] . . . Heifer Project where they gave cattle to help Europeans restore their agricultural base."

Traveling around Europe with Brethren became his foreign policy training. "I did not take a single course in foreign policy or international affairs in school," he said. "While I traveled I developed my whole sense of mission that the world could be changed without violence."

This commitment to nonviolence was sorely tested early in his ministry after he was asked as a young pastor to help organize a voter's registration drive in Georgia. The Klan began to organize against his work, and Young told his wife (he and Jean were married in 1954) to watch any confrontation between him and the Klan from a window with a rifle in hand. She refused.

"I would never point a rifle at a human being," Young recalled her saying. "If you don't believe all this stuff about the cross and resurrection, we should pack up and go home."

"I thought to myself, I've married a woman who really and truly believes this."

At the 1977 Annual Conference in Richmond, Virginia, Young remarked, "My first diplomatic experience was the six weeks I spent in a Brethren workcamp in Austria with representatives of some twenty different nations, and the travels through Europe with Brethren Volunteer Service in the early 1950s. In this I discerned that diplomacy was not just a matter of principles and treaties and ideals, but essentially a people-to-people phenomenon."

For the rest of his life, Young decided to learn about countries by talking to the people and not by taking the word of experts.

Later, as part of Jimmy Carter's administration, he recalled, "The CIA was always at odds with me about what was going on in Africa. I was getting my views from Africans and missionaries. Fortunately, Jimmy Carter was enough of a Christian to listen to me."

In the speech at Camp Mack, Young made this point: "The traditions from Camp Mack and Manchester College gave me the grounding that springs from the life of the church, which is revealed by people in small groups by the presence and power of the Holy Spirit, and that power can change the world in which we live without violence.

"Camp Mack along with King's Mountain shaped my life and put me on a track so that I have found answers for every challenge my life has faced, and I haven't had to do anything but open my heart and mind to the Spirit of the Living God," he continued. "God will meet you, mold you, fill you, and use you. I have been in the presence of miracles. As you bring people here in the presence of the Spirit, miracles will continue to be wrought. We will continue to grow in grace and glory. Thank you for helping me find this path."

# A WALK ALONG THE ATLANTIC— OR IS IT THE PACIFIC?

**28**

**JILL EIKENBERRY • 1947-**

*The famous Hollywood actor is walking along the shore of the Atlantic Ocean* in Europe from where the Brethren began their trek across the trackless ocean in 1719, then on the East Coast of the United States, where the Brethren landed months later to begin their new lives.

But this is film, and the actor is actually walking along the Pacific Coast in a quiet cove near her home in the San Francisco area.

It's hard to imagine that old chestnut—"What's a nice girl like you doing in a place like this?"—working as a pickup line, but it seems like it would have been the right question to ask actor Jill Eikenberry, who appeared in the video *By Water and the Word: The Birth of the Brethren* (1996).

Eikenberry's appearance was arranged by her cousin, Glenn Timmons, who at the time was a General Board executive. Although the background footage and interviews were taped in Germany and the Netherlands during the 1995 Brethren Heritage Tour led by Donald and Hedda Durnbaugh (and itself the subject of a Sollenberger video), Eikenberry's narration along with the opening and closing sequences were performed as a favor to Timmons, as a way to give back to her Brethren heritage.

Our Brethren historians appear in the video one by one: Jeff Bach, Donald F. Durnbaugh, Bill Willoughby, and others. It tells the tale of the Pietist separatists, the hardships they endured, the risks they took, and, finally, their trip to a new world where they could practice their faith as they chose.

But it is Eikenberry who becomes the face and voice of the story of Brethren beginnings as she uses her talents to engage the viewer in what is a complex and compelling story of faith and promise. A native of New Haven, Connecticut, and raised in Madison, Wisconsin, and St. Joseph and Kansas City, Missouri, she is known for her role as Ann Kelsey in the television series *L.A. Law,* which ran from 1986 to 1994 and featured her husband/actor, Michael Tucker, as well. She has also performed in films and on the Broadway stage. In the late eighties, Eikenberry discovered that she had breast cancer. Her treatment over the following two years was successful, and she subsequently co-produced the documentary *Destined to Live,* which features cancer survivors and for which she won a Humanitas Award. She also won a Golden Globe Award in 1988 for *L.A. Law*.

Freelance video producer David Sollenberger of Annville, Pennsylvania, wrote the script for *By Water and the Word* and produced and edited the film as well. David qualifies for celebrity status, too, because he is ever present, ever working for the advancement and benefit of the church. Though working most often behind the scenes, you'll see him at major

Brethren events, camera resting on his shoulder, filming, interviewing. His writing rarely appears between the covers of a book or magazine, but it has helped shape the interpretation of our story through the many films that have appeared at Annual Conference on behalf of every Brethren agency. It has been his guiding hand that has made so much of the filmed Brethren story professional, compelling, and clear.

In 1995 Sollenberger was part of the major Brethren Heritage Tour in Europe led by Don Durnbaugh. "I shot the travelogue and went along on that tour with this project in mind," he said. The trip provided many of the background shots that would be used in the film.

Once back in the United States, David set to work. "I wrote the entire script and figured out what part Jill Eikenberry was going to do on camera and what part she was going to read." The script was reviewed by a historical committee that included Don Durnbaugh, Ken Shaffer, and several others, to ensure its accuracy.

Sollenberger was impressed by Eikenberry's professionalism. "She was just an incredibly talented woman who was able to take that script, read it, and then perform it on camera perfectly." Though there were three or four takes for every shot, he insisted that he could have used any one of them.

"The ocean and the wind were the real problem," David remembered. "I was always living in fear that my microphone would fail. But everything turned out nicely, and it was a fabulous job." The off-camera narration was recorded at Eikenberry's home before the outdoor shoot.

"She was very gracious and cooperative about the whole thing," Sollenberger said. "This was her way of giving back to her roots. She was really appreciative of her Brethren heritage and this opportunity to give back."

*The One About*

# THE FLY-FISHING COMMISSIONER OF THE FDA

**JANE E. HENNEY • CA. 1948-**

29

*She loves fly-fishing, reads books of all sorts, cooks, gardens, works out at the local fitness club combining two of her passions of weight lifting and yoga,* is married, and shares her home with a long-haired dachshund named Stover. And along the way she was the first woman to serve as the commissioner of the U.S. Food and Drug Administration (FDA).

The "Brethren Brush" with Jane E. Henney, a native of Woodburn, Indiana, began at Manchester College. "My father went to Manchester College," she recalls, "and I had attended homecoming events, etc., with him and my mother many times when I was growing up." She herself chose to go to Manchester because "I wanted an experience at a college of a manageable size rather than a huge university. Manchester was also far enough away from home that I could have my independence, yet close enough to my home that it wasn't a major undertaking to go home when I needed to. I also knew that Manchester had a strong pre-med/science program."

Henney lists her favorite Manchester faculty as "Dr. Emerson Niswander, Mrs. Onita Johnson, Dr. Eberly, Dr. Opurt, Dr. Weimer, and Dr. Ken Brown." After receiving her undergraduate degree from Manchester College, she went on to get a medical degree from Indiana University and then focused on medical oncology at the University of Texas M. D. Anderson Cancer Center and at the National Cancer Institute.

When asked what influence the Brethren might have had on her during her years at Manchester College, Henney noted, "During the time I was at Manchester, the Vietnam War was at its peak." She called to mind "the Brethren philosophy/values . . . of alternative service rather than participation in military operations. Thus, the war and support or lack thereof by those of the Brethren faith was quite evident."

Over the years she worked at the National Cancer Institute at the National Institutes of Health, specializing in the Cancer Therapy and Evaluation Program. She was first brought into the FDA during the Clinton administration from 1992 to 1994, serving as deputy commissioner for operations; then she went to work at the University of New Mexico as vice president of the health sciences center.

In 1998 she was named the first woman to serve as the commissioner of the FDA, a position she held until 2001.

One of her biggest aims, Henney said, was "assuring that the Agency's decisions regarding product reviews, policy matters, or enforcement actions were based on science." It was important, Henney added, to be "working on public health issues that were/are important, i.e., new product approvals (drugs and devices), the safety of the blood supply, food safety."

Her greatest frustration was "having insufficient resources to get the job done. . . . The FDA is a chronically under-resourced yet greatly needed agency of government."

Today Henney is the senior vice president and provost for Health Affairs at the University of Cincinnati. "Working at an academic health center provides the opportunity to train the next generation of health professionals (doctors, nurses, pharmacists, and other therapists), oversee biomedical research that may result in new approaches to treatments, and participate in the development of new platforms of care. I love the complexity of the organization and the opportunity to make a difference in the health and well-being of the community."

Dr. Henney has received many awards and honors, including election to the National Academy of Science Institute of Medicine, the Society of Medical Administrators, and honorary membership in the American College of Health Care Executives. She received the Excellence in Women's Health Award from The Jacobs Institute, the Public Health Leadership Award from the National Organization of Rare Disorders, the Department of Health and Human Services Secretary's Recognition Award, and the Public Health Service Commendation Medal twice.

The fly-fishing is something new for Dr. Henney, but she tries to remain open to new experiences.

# THE ARTIST WHO TRADED HIS MICROSCOPE FOR A PAINT BRUSH—AND BECAME FAMOUS

## 30

**CHRIS RASCHKA • 1959-**

*Like many young people with a newly minted and expensive college diploma in hand, Chris Durnbaugh weighed his options and tried to make a sensible choice.* A talented musician and artist with an affinity for science, he had just received a degree in biology from St. Olaf College in Minnesota. The most sensible thing was to apply for medical school, which he did.

Then he struggled with second thoughts and literally at the last minute made a life-changing decision: "The morning of my first day of medical school, I called the school and told them I wasn't going to come. That's when I knew I really wanted to be a painter."

WESTMINSTER DRIVE

10' GRASS

EXISTING EL. POLE

5' WALKWAY

Once Chris decided to skip medical school, he figured he needed to tell his folks, Brethren historians Don and Hedda Durnbaugh. According to a story he told at the Brethren Press breakfast at the 2007 Annual Conference, his father was busy in his office "writing the Brethren Encyclopedia. I told him what I was doing; he nodded and hurriedly said, 'That's fine,' and went back to writing the encyclopedia." After the laughter subsided, Chris added that his parents always supported his decision.

Chris was born in Pennsylvania in 1959, and when he was three years old he moved with his parents to Lombard, Illinois. He grew up around Bethany Theological Seminary, where his father taught Brethren history. His mother, Hedwig Raschka, met Don while she was in a refugee camp in Austria following World War II and he was a Brethren Service worker who had been anointed by M. R. Zigler as *the* future Brethren historian. Don and Hedda worked together on the ground-breaking source book *European Origins of the Brethren,* published by Brethren Press in 1958, which provided the facts that swept away the myths of Brethren beginnings.

You might be wondering how Chris Durnbaugh became known as Chris Raschka, the writer and illustrator of children's books. The choice to use his mother's maiden name was made together by Chris and his wife, Lydie. "I was like a lot of other Brethren young people in the seventies. When we decided to get married, Lydie and I wanted to have the same name, but we didn't like the idea of automatically taking my father's name." Though they originally thought of putting the four surnames of their parents into a hat and pulling one out, they realized they both liked Raschka best.

Having decided against medical school, Raschka still needed a job. Though the classified ads in most newspapers don't include a section for artists, he did find and get a position as a paralegal, which led to regular work illustrating the *Michigan Bar Journal.* But his desire to pursue a career in art led him and his young family to New York.

Raschka's first major book, *Charlie Parker Played Be Bop*, was published in 1992 by Orchard Press. In appreciation for the great jazz artist's music, Raschka mixes drawings of dancing shoes, marching birds, and other fanciful creatures with an arch cat and the great cat Charlie Parker, enhanced by an engaging text that replicates Parker's rhythms and the repeated warning, "Never leave your cat alone." Another book, *Mysterious Thelonious,* illustrates the monochromatic techniques of the great Theolonious Monk across a multi-colored grid with a text that insists, "There were no wrong notes on his piano." To this date Raschka has written and/or illustrated more than forty children's books.

For the book *I Pledge Allegiance,* which he illustrated, Raschka notes on the back flap, "My parents have always respectfully refused to recite the Pledge of Allegiance—for religious reasons and reasons of personal experience. That's why I was drawn to this project. In America, we each have the freedom to choose, including the freedom to choose whether or not to say the Pledge."

Books published by Brethren Press include his very first book, the Cold War parable entitled *R and Я: A Story About Two Alphabets* (1990). He also illustrated *Benjamin Brody's Backyard Bag* (1991), a book on homelessness, and *This I Remember* (1995), a remembrance by Juniata College professor emeritus George Dolnikowski, who left Russia during World War II and resettled in the U.S. through the help of the Brethren. When Raschka illustrated *Benjamin Brody's Backyard Bag,* he depicted the homeless person as white and the helpful middle-class family as black in order to challenge the assumptions of many of his readers. Raschka has also illustrated two children's books written and published by Brethren author Jim Lehman: *The Saga of Shakespeare Pintlewood* (1990) and *The Owl and the Tuba* (1991).

A writer/illustrator's life is a precarious one. Prizes and official recognition can provide a little security at the least. In 1994 Raschka's *Yo? Yes!* was named a Caldecott Honor Book, which led to more work from publishers. In 2006 he won the Caldecott Medal for his illustrations of Norton Juster's *The Hello-Goodbye Window,* an endearing story of a little girl's visits to er grandparents' house. "He's so different and venturesome. He's absolutely fearless," said Juster, who is also author of the classic *The Phantom Tollbooth*. "The book has such a life because of his illustrations."

Raschka was out when the phone call arrived from the Caldecott Medal committee, so he received word on his message machine. He called the award "a great thrill" and noted that the message stayed on his machine for quite a long time. He added that winning the award is "a little daunting, though it's a little like carrying a beautiful pebble in your pocket. I can take it out and look at it, and it calms me down."

The award, given by a division of the American Library Association to "the artist of the most distinguished American picture book for children," led to an appearance on NBC's *Today* show as well as an interview on National Public Radio and much greater recognition for his work.

Among the many influences on his work, Raschka points to Brethren minister and artist Paul Grout who, while a student at Bethany Seminary, taught a weekly art class at York Center Church of the Brethren in Lombard, Illinois. Chris also credits his father, Don, as an influence: "My father was a very artistic person, although he would have denied it." He recalls how Don would bring home "found objects" from his walk and put them together into artistic constructions.

Raschka and his family are currently members of Trinity Lutheran Church in New York, but he credits his Brethren roots, among other things, for aspects of his work, such as his commitment to justice and racial equality. When asked by an interviewer if he ever regretted abandoning a career in medicine for the insecure life of an artist, Raschka replied, "No. I feel extremely lucky. I wouldn't trade this for anything else."

# THE BRETHREN FELLOW WHO GOES THE DISTANCE

**31**

**BRIAN SELL • 1978-**

*If you have ever run community distance events, you have probably seen the t-shirt with the saying on the back that reads simply, "There is no finish line."*

Long-distance running is a popular hobby across the United States, but there are those special souls who not only run the marathon, but run it so well that they can run sub-five-minute-miles forever—or least for 26 miles, 385 yards, the distance of the marathon.

Brian Sell, born and raised in the Woodbury (Pa.) Church of the Brethren, is one of those people, but he is not considered a natural talent. Elite runner Dathan

Ritzenhein, in an interview with mensracing.com, spoke about the many talented runners in the United States, but added, "I don't want to say anything about [Brian Sell]—but we have a lot more talent, probably, straight off the boards, and maybe we don't have to run 160 miles a week to get to that same level. I really admire [Sell] and those guys, because it doesn't come quite as easy for them."

Brian wouldn't argue with Ritzenhein. That's why he runs an average of 130 miles a week, or close to 5,000 miles a year. He's determined to do the best he can.

When asked in an interview for this book how his Brethren background helps him in his running, he said, "I think, like most Brethren people, I speak softly and carry a big stick. . . . A lot of people have big mouths and like to brag about what they've done and what they're going to do. I've kind of learned from my Brethren upbringing to keep my mouth shut and let my race to do my talking for me and remain humble. You've got to give everything back to God."

Brian Sell was a high school standout for his area, but his 10:06 two-mile personal record is considered modest at best. He attended Saint Francis University, a relatively unknown small college in rural Pennsylvania, where he met his wife, Sarah, when both were teammates on the cross-country team. Sarah comes from the Lititz Church of the Brethren.

Since 2001 Brian has been a member of the Hansons-Brooks Distance Project, based in the state of Michigan. Although he considers running his "primary job," he still works part-time at Home Depot.

Over the years Brian has become a world-class marathoner, entering the ranks of the elite runners because of his tenacity and hard work. To him it's important to be part of a team. "It helps to have a group of guys to meet up with every day. I tried to do it on my own in Pennsylvania over a summer, and it was just real tough to get myself motivated."

He ran in the 2004 Olympic trials and led until mile 22. "I hit the wall pretty hard," he admits, but he said that event—

he eventually finished twelfth—cemented his love for the distance. "I realized the marathon was the way to go." The reason? "The harder you work, the better you get at it. It has a lot more work-success ratio than most races. Shorter races are more of a talent factor. The marathon is putting the miles in. I can run slower miles for a long time."

"Slower miles" is all relative. In the 2006 Boston Marathon, Sell's time was 2:10:55, which works out to a 4:59 per mile pace. That put him in a special class worthy of notice. "I think my Boston race in 2006 was my best. I was fourth there. I ran a personal best, pretty tough course, and a pretty fast time. I felt good doing it."

For him consistency is the key, as is race planning. "I think the big thing is just preparing yourself for the 20-mile mark. That's where the race really begins. Most of the guys feel pretty good for 20 miles. Then it's a totally different race. Your legs don't work like you're used to. You start seeing some things you don't normally see."

In order to keep going at that point, Brian says he focuses on just a few things: "Pretty much getting it done. I start thinking about the training I've done and concentrate on putting one foot in front of the other, not letting your pace fall back."

As he trained for the November 2007 Olympic trials for the 2008 Beijing Olympics, Sell put things in perspective: "I still consider myself a strong Brethren, and my wife and I are going to go back to the Woodbury Church within the next year and a half depending on how the trials come out."

Postscript: On November 3, 2007, Brian Sell fulfilled his dream of qualifying for the Olympics, running 2:11:40 and finishing third, behind two much younger runners. With the third place finish, he earned a place on the 2008 Olympic team. The following remarks were recorded in an interview for the *Bedford* (Pa.) *Gazette* (Spring).

"It's been thirteen years in the making for me, so this is one of the greatest days of my life aside from the birth of my daughter [Lily Grace]," Brian said afterwards. And he was quick in the interview to praise others, saying of those who finished ahead of him, "The future of distance running looks great for these guys. They're tough in the marathon and they're young. The future looks bright."

The race took place in New York and, after a start near Times Square, featured five long laps around Central Park. It was a cold and windy day, which affected times. Early in the race Brian decided he'd have to stay with the front pack no matter what happened.

"The original plan was to let the field determine the pace for the first couple of miles. When we were out in 11 [minutes] flat for two miles, I knew I had to keep it honest to have a chance at all. Honestly, I was trying to run around five flat per mile. I didn't have too many miles above five flat. That tells you how fast these guys were up front."

Brian decided to "keep relaxed until the last lap, then attack. . . . I'm just happy I timed it right." He ended up finishing nearly a minute ahead of the fourth place runner and called it "a dream come true."

# THE MAN WHO RAN IN CIRCLES TO FIND HIMSELF IN THE WINNER'S CIRCLE

**32**

**SAM HORNISH, JR. • 1979-**

*How do you get to the Winner's Circle at the Indianapolis Speedway?*

Go fast. Turn left . . .

Of course, if it were *that* easy a lot more folks would take their turn at drinking the milk they give you after winning the Indianapolis 500. It takes skill, training, endurance, a great car, a great team, some luck—and sometimes an eyelash!

Which is about how much of a lead Sam Hornish, Jr., had when he won the race in 2006.

When our Middle Pennsylvania District bus caravan stopped to take a tour of the Indianapolis

Speedway on our way to National Youth Conference a couple of months after that race, it was with pride that I pointed to an exhibit touting the most recent winner and said to the youth, "Did you know that Sam Hornish, Jr., is a member of the Church of the Brethren?"

Hornish grew up in the Poplar Ridge Church of the Brethren in Defiance, Ohio, and was baptized at the age of nine by Glen Whisler, who was pastor there at the time. (Whisler would later officiate when Hornish married his wife, Crystal, in 2004.)

Sam's mother figured that one day he'd grow up to become either a minister or a race car driver. (Truth be told, he probably picked the safer profession.)

"I don't remember ever missing church growing up except for the occasional family vacation," Hornish recalled when he spoke to the Roann (Ind.) congregation early in 2007. "We lived about thirty miles away from church and made the drive every Sunday."

Hornish made sure to bring a friend whenever possible, especially those who did not attend a church. He was a faithful attendee until, at age eleven, he began racing go-karts under his father's supervision. For the two Sam's— Jr. and Sr.— it began as a weekend hobby that soon gobbled up a larger chunk of the year. Even so, he kept his connection to the church.

"I would call my grandmother to see what the message was, or I'd listen to a service on the radio. Or my Dad would have me read a passage from the Bible. I always had a Bible with me; I always carried a small one in my bag."

As Sam approached his teen years, it was more difficult sometimes to get up on a Sunday morning, but he always tried to go to worship. "Teenagers usually stay up late Saturday night playing video games, watching movies, and doing other things." While admitting that teens need to do some of these things, he insisted that it's important to "make sure you wake up and get to the church the next morning. That's truly the important thing in life."

As he became more serious about his career, he typically found it necessary on a race day to fulfill commitments to his sponsors when he wasn't actually preparing for the race, but he made a point of attending church services that are available at the track on race day. "That's the time I can sit there and not think about racing. I can go to the service and spend a half hour thinking about God and thinking about my family, the important things in life."

Sam entered his first Indy Racing League (IRL) IndyCar Series event in 2000 and quickly made a name for himself. He was one of the top drivers and, during his first six years racing on the IRL circuit, Sam took home the season-long championship three times. But his lifelong goal, winning the Indianapolis 500, eluded him until 2006.

The victory was anything but inevitable. He won the pole position in the time trials, but by the end of the first lap he had already fallen behind. There are 200 laps, each 2.5 miles long, in the event, and Hornish led at the end of only 19 of them.

By the end of the 25th lap, Hornish found himself seven seconds behind, in third place. Astute work in his pit stop led to his retaking second place by the 38th lap, but he continued to fall farther behind, 12 seconds by lap 56 and 15 seconds by lap 61.

Things got worse in the 66th lap, when a caution flag led to Hornish taking to the pits again, going in second, but coming out fourth. It wasn't until the 78th lap that he worked his way back to third, and, finally, by the halfway point he was at least battling for second with another driver.

However, Sam fell to fifth place in lap 108 and only gradually would work his way back into contention in second place.

On lap 151 disaster nearly struck. Hornish drove away from the pits with the fuel nozzle stuck in his car, spraying a member of his crew with gas, who was then doused with water by the rest of his crew. Hornish stopped and the nozzle was removed, but he fell to eighth, and within four laps was given the penalty of driving through Pit Road at 60 miles an hour.

Roger Penske, the team owner, made a critical decision: Hornish would use the penalty on lap 161 as an opportunity to refuel so he could go the rest of the race without stopping. By the time refueling was complete, he was 29 seconds behind the leader, and the last car on the lead lap.

Then slowly Hornish began to close the gap, going from eighth to sixth, to fifth and by lap 193 fourth place. On lap 197 Hornish passed two cars to move into second, but his attempt to take first place in lap 199 was foiled by the leader, Marco Andretti, who cut him off and forced him to lose momentum.

Finally, on the third turn of the final lap he found himself on Andretti's tail, and as the two headed out of the fourth and final turn of the final lap Hornish slipped by Andretti to win the race by 0.0635 of a second, which was the second closest finish in the race's history. The sling-shot effect of passing Andretti made him the first driver ever in the ninety years of running the race to take the lead and win in that last lap.

That victory was part of his third IndyLeague win in six years. And it was only the eighteenth time someone won the race starting in the pole position.

Races come and go, but a victory at Indianapolis is lasting. So is Hornish's commitment to his Christian faith and ministry. His winnings have enabled him to establish the Sam Hornish Jr. Foundation to do charitable outreach. He and his wife also currently serve on the IRL Ministry's board of directors.

# SELECTED LIST OF WORKS CONSULTED

### 1. Benjamin Franklin

Brumbaugh, Martin Grove. *A History of the German Baptist Brethren in Europe and America.* Mount Morris, Ill.: Brethren Publishing House, 1899.

Durnbaugh, Donald F., ed. *The Brethren in Colonial America.* Elgin, Ill.: Brethren Press, 1967.

Eller, Vernard. "A Tale of Two Printers—One City." *Brethren Life and Thought* 16, vol. 1 (1971).

Franklin, Benjamin. *Autobiography.* First English publication, 1793.

Longenecker, Stephen L. *The Christopher Sauers.* Elgin, Ill.: Brethren Press, 1981.

"Wohlfahrt, Michael." *The Brethren Encyclopedia.* 4 vols. Philadelphia, Pa.: The Brethren Encyclopedia, Inc., 1983-2005.

### 2. George Washington

Morse, Kenneth I. "George Washington Came with His Dinner." *The Brethren Encyclopedia.* 4 vols. Philadelphia, Pa.: The Brethren Encyclopedia, Inc., 1983-2005: 1320 (sidebar).

Morse, Kenneth I. *Preaching in a Tavern.* Elgin, Ill.: Brethren Press, 1997.

Quinter, James. "Our Visit to Virginia." *The Primitive Christian and the Pilgrim* 2, vol. 21 (1878).

*Rare Newspapers.* http://www.rarenewspapers.com.

### 3. Daniel Boone

"Boone, Daniel." *The Brethren Encyclopedia.* 4 vols. Philadelphia, Pa.: The Brethren Encyclopedia, Inc., 1983-2006.

Flory, Rolland F. *Lest We Forget and Tales of Yester-Years, Volume III.* Springfield, Ohio, 1976.

### 4. Harriet Livermore

Brumbaugh, Martin Grove. *A History of the German Baptist Brethren in Europe and America.* Mount Morris, Ill.: Brethren Publishing House, 1899.

Livermore, S. T. *Harriet Livermore: The "Pilgrim Stranger."* Hartford, Conn.: Case, Lockwood and Brainard Co., 1884.

Morse, Kenneth I. *Preaching in a Tavern.* Elgin, Ill.: Brethren Press, 1997.

Morse, Kenneth I. "Vixen or Devotee?" *The Brethren Encyclopedia.* 4 vols. Philadelphia, Pa.: The Brethren Encyclopedia, Inc., 1983-2006: 750-51 (sidebar).

## 5. John Clement Studebaker and family

Carlock, Walter, Alvin Faust, Irene Miller, Ruth Studebaker, and Emmert Studebaker. *The Studebaker Family in America*. The Studebaker Family National Association, 1976, 1986.

Durnbaugh, Donald F. *Fruit of the Vine*. Elgin, Ill.: Brethren Press, 1997.

Morse, Kenneth I. "More Than You Promise: the Studebakers." *The Brethren Encyclopedia*. 4 vols. Philadelphia, Pa.: The Brethren Encyclopedia, Inc., 1983-2006: 1230 (sidebar).

*The Studebaker Family*. The Studebaker Family National Association 27 (1971).

Thomasson, Kermon. Letter to the author. August 11, 2007.

## 6. Abraham Lincoln

Martin, Jim. "The Secret Baptism of Abraham Lincoln." *Restoration Quarterly* 38, vol. 2 (1996).

Morse, Kenneth I. "A Secret Baptism." *The Brethren Encyclopedia*. 4 vols. Philadelphia, Pa.: The Brethren Encyclopedia, Inc., 1983-2006: 743 (sidebar).

Morse, Kenneth I. *Preaching in a Tavern*. Elgin, Ill.: Brethren Press, 1997.

## 7. William H. Rinehart

Doxzen, Duane. "William H. Rinehart Exhibit." *Carroll County Times*, April 30, 1995.

Doxzen, Duane. "William H. Rinehart: American Sculptor." The Historical Society of Carroll County, Maryland. http://hscc.carr.org/exhibitions/Rinehart.htm.

Morse, Kenneth I. *Preaching in a Tavern*. Elgin, Ill.: Brethren Press, 1997.

Morse, Kenneth I. "William T. Rinehart: American Sculptor." *The Brethren Encyclopedia*. 4 vols. Philadelphia, Pa.: The Brethren Encyclopedia, Inc., 1983-2006: 1109-110 (sidebar).

## 8. John T. Lewis

Morse, Kenneth I. "John T. Lewis, Friend of Mark Twain." *The Brethren Encyclopedia*. 4 vols. Philadelphia, Pa.: The Brethren Encyclopedia, Inc., 1983-2006: 851 (sidebar).

"The Tale of a Dunkard Bible Gone Astray." *The Inglenook*, May 1, 1906.

Wisbey, Herbert A., Jr. "John T. Lewis, Mark Twain's Friend in Elmira." *Mark Twain Society Bulletin* 7, vol. 1 (1984).

Wisbey, Robert D., and Herbert A. Wisbey, Jr. *Mark Twain in Elmira*. Mark Twain Society, 1977.

Thomasson, Kermon. "Mark Twain and His Dunker Friend." *Messenger,* October 1985.

### 9. Susan McSween Barber

Chamberlain, Kathleen P. "In the Shadow of Billy the Kid: Susan McSween and the Lincoln County War." *Montana (The Magazine of Western History)*, Winter 2005. Montana Historical Society. Brethren Historical Library and Archives collection.

### 10. David Emmert

Morse, Kenneth I. *Preaching in a Tavern*. Elgin, Ill.: Bethren Press, 1997.

Morse, Kenneth I. "David Emmert: Artist and Inventor." *The Brethren Encyclopedia*. 4 vols. Philadelphia, Pa.: The Brethren Encyclopedia, Inc., 1983-2006: 235 (sidebar).

### 11. Phoebe Ann Mosey/"Annie Oakley"

Flory, Claude R. "M. G. Wants Me for a Sunbeam." *Brethren Life and Thought* 21, vol. 2 (1976).

Morse, Kenneth I. *Preaching in a Tavern*. Elgin, Ill.: Brethren Press, 1997.

Morse, Kenneth I. "An Oakley from Ohio." *The Brethren Encyclopedia*. 4 vols. Philadelphia, Pa.: The Brethren Encyclopedia, Inc., 1983-2006: 958 (sidebar).

### 12. Martin Grove Brumbaugh

Durnbaugh, Donald F. "Martin Grove Brumbaugh, the 'Pioneer Brethren Historian' and His Rivals." Paper presented at the Brethren Historical Committee Insight Session, Annual Conference 1999.

Flory, Claude R. "M. G. Wants Me for a Sunbeam." *Brethren Life and Thought* 21, vol. 2 (1976).

Brumbaugh, Martin Grove. Biographical files, Brethren Historical Library and Archives collection. Elgin, Illinois.

Morse, Kenneth I. "The Making of a Brumbaugh." *The Brethren Encyclopedia*. 4 vols. Philadelphia, Pa.: The Brethren Encyclopedia, Inc., 1983-2006: 223 (sidebar).

"Personality and Career of Martin Grove Brumbaugh." *Philadelphia "Public Ledger,"* March 22, 1914.

### 13. Emma Nice Ellis

Morse, Kenneth I. *Preaching in a Tavern*. Elgin: Brethren Press, 1997.

Zigler, M. R. Interview with Mrs. Charles Calvert Ellis, July 24, 1963. Brethren Historical Library and Archives collection, Elgin, Illinois.

## 14. Myra Brooks Welch

Gilbert, Mrs. J. Z. [Welch sidebar]. *The Gospel Messenger*, December 28, 1935.

Hollinger, Mrs. Albert. "The Story of a Poem." *The Gospel Messenger*, November 7, 1959.

"La Verne Woman Traced as Author of Poem." *Los Angeles Times*, December 27, 1953.

McFadden, Wendy. *The Story Behind the Touch of the Master's Hand.* Elgin, Ill.: Brethren Press, 1997.

Morse, Kenneth I. *Preaching in a Tavern*. Elgin, Ill.: Brethren Press, 1997.

Thomasson, Kermon. "A Poem for Lives Out of Tune." *Messenger*, February 1981.

"Welch, Myra Brooks." *The Brethren Encyclopedia*. 4 vols. Philadelphia, Pa.: The Brethren Encyclopedia, Inc., 1983-2006.

## 15. Anna Evans Wilson

Correspondence between Dr. Ray A. Neff and Kermon Thomasson, July 27, 1985, and August 2, 1985. Brethren Historical Library and Archives collection, Elgin, Illinois.

Thomasson, Kermon. "Page One." *Messenger*, February 1985.

## 16. Laura Wine

"Brethren in the News: Laura Wine." *Messenger*, March 27, 1969.

Fuller, John G. *Fever! The Hunt for a New Killer Virus.* New York: Readers Digest Press, 1974.

Hamer, John and Esther. "Lassa Fever: The Story of a Killer Virus." *Messenger*, July 1974.

"Retired Nurse Now Serves in Garkida Hospital." *The Gospel Messenger*, December 5, 1964.

Thomasson, Kermon. Correspondence with the author, August 11, 2007.

## 17. Andrew W. Cordier

"Cordier, Andrew Wellington." *The Brethren Encyclopedia*. 4 vols. Philadelphia, Pa.: The Brethren Encyclopedia, Inc., 1983-2006.

Cordier, Andrew W. "Challenge in the Congo." *Think*, July-August 1965.

Cordier, Andrew W. "The Role of the Secretary-General." Address given May 15, 1961. Reprinted from the *Annual Review of United Nations Affairs 1960-61*. Ed., Richard N. Swift. New York: Oceana Publications, 1961.

Cordier, Andrew W. "The United Nations in a World of Tension and Change." Reprinted from *South Dakota Law Review* 7 (Spring 1962).

Dedication program for the Cordier Auditorium, Manchester College, September 23, 1978.

"Memorial Tribute to Andrew Wellington Cordier 1901-1975." *Manchester College Bulletin*, December 1975.

"The UN at 25: A Conversation with Andrew W. Cordier." *Messenger*, October 22, 1970.

### 18. Nathan Leopold

Leopold, Nathan. Biographical files, Brethren Historical Library and Archives collection, Elgin, Illinois.

Morse, Kenneth I., and Leona Z. Row Eller. "The Companionship, the Acceptance." *The Brethren Encyclopedia*. 4 vols. Philadelphia, Pa.: The Brethren Encyclopedia, Inc., 1983-2006: 738 (sidebar).

Royer, Howard. "Nathan Leopold Calls on the Brethren." *The Gospel Messenger*, February 1, 1964.

Willoughby, Lena B. "The Leopold I Knew." *Bridgewater Alumni*, November 1971.

### 19. Roy J. Plunkett

"Teflon, at Age 50, Will Stick around." *Chicago Tribune*, April 11, 1988.

Plunkett, Roy. Biographical files, Brethren Historical Library and Archives collection, Elgin, Illinois.

### 20. Paul John Flory

Chemistry Symposium [program], October 24, 1975. Manchester College Chemistry Department.

Flory, Paul John. Biographical files, Brethren Historical Library and Archives collection, Elgin, Illinois.

"Flory, Paul John." *The Brethren Encyclopedia*. 4 vols. Philadelphia, Pa.: The Brethren Encyclopedia, Inc., 1983-2006.

"Nobel Prize: Paul Flory, the Nobel Prize in Chemistry 1974–Autobiography." Nobel Prize.org. http://nobelprize.org/nobel_prizes/chemistry/laureates/1974/flory-autobio.html.

"Nobel Prize: Paul Flory, the Nobel Prize in Chemistry 1974–Banquet Speech." Nobelprize.org. http://nobelprize.org/nobel_prizes/chemistry/laureates/1974/flory-speech.html.

### 21. William Stafford

"Stafford, William." *The Brethren Encyclopedia*. 4 vols. Philadelphia, Pa.: The Brethren Encyclopedia, Inc., 1983-2006.

Stafford, William. *A Scripture of Leaves*. Elgin, Ill.: Brethren Press, 1989, 1999.

Stafford, William. *Down in My Heart*. Elgin, Ill.: Brethren Press, 1947, 1971.

Williamstafford.org. http://www.williamstafford.org.

**22. Paul Hume**

Ferrell, Robert H., ed. *Off the Record: The Private Papers of Harry S. Truman.* Harper and Row, 1980.

Hume obituary. *Washington Post*, November 27, 2001.

McCullough, David. *Truman.* New York: Simon and Schuster, 1992.

Truman, Margaret. *Harry S. Truman.* New York: William Morrow and Company, Inc., 1973.

**23. Otis "Slim" Whitman**

Gibble, Kenneth. *Mr. Songman: The Slim Whitman Story.* Elgin, Ill.: Brethren Press, 1982.

**24. Bob Richards**

Alden, Robert. "Richards Reaches Heights in Pole Vaulting Victory." *New York Times*, November 27, 1956.

"Bob Richards: The Five-Second Champion." *Bridgewater*, Winter 2007.

"Champions of Breakfast Cereal." *Rocky Mountain News*, November 22, 1994.

"Executives: Health, Wealth, and Wheaties." *U.S. Business*, June 16, 1967.

Frank, Stanley. "The Sky's the Limit." *Redbook Magazine*, July 1952.

Morse, Kenneth I. "Pole-Vaulting Preacher." *The Brethren Encyclopedia*. 4 vols. Philadelphia, Pa.: The Brethren Encyclopedia, Inc., 1983-2006: 70 (sidebar).

Paxton, Harry T. "That Big-Talking, Pole-Vaulting Parson." *Saturday Evening Post*, (n.d.).

**25. Don Murray**

Kreider, J. Kenneth. *A Cup of Cold Water*. Elgin, Ill.: Brethren Press, 2001.

Murray, Don. Biographical files, Brethren Historical Library and Archives collection, Elgin, Illinois.

Murray, Don. "I Had to Find My Own Way of Fighting." *The Gospel Messenger*, January 7, 1958.

Murray, Don. Phone interview with the author, May 23, 2007.

Murray, Don. "The People Nobody Wanted." *The Gospel Messenger*, November 4, 1961.

**26. James Earl Jones**

Jones, James Earl, and Penelope Niven. *Voices and Silences*. Charles Scribner's Sons, 1993.

Morse, Kenneth I. *Preaching in a Tavern*. Elgin, Ill.: Brethren Press, 1997.

Wiltschek, Walt. "How a Brethren Teacher Gave Voice to a Famous Voice." *Messenger*, January/February 2003.

**27. Andrew Young and Jean Childs Young**

"Former Ambassador Speaks in Milford." *The Goshen News*,
    May 21, 2000.

"Jean Young (1933-1994)." *The Atlanta Journal/The Atlantic
    Constitution*, September 17, 1994.

Young, Andrew/Jean. Biographical files, Brethren Historical
    Library and Archives collection, Elgin, Illinois.

Radio interview. "Midmorning with Kerri Miller." Minnesota Public
    Radio, February 21, 2007.

**28. Jill Eikenberry**

"Jill Eikenberry and Michael Tucker." Tuckerberry.com.
    http://www.tuckerberry.com. (2007).

Sollenberger, David. E-mail interview with the author,
    summer 2007.

**29. Jane E. Henney**

"Dr. Jane Henney: Biography." *Pew Initiative on Food and
    Biotechnology*. http://pewagbiotech.org/events/0717/
    henney.php. (2007).

Henney, Jane E. E-mail interview with the author, May 21, 2007.

**30. Chris Raschka**

"Chris Raschka: Biography." Hyperion Books for Children.com.
    http://www.hyperionbooksforchildren.com/authors/
    displayAI.asp?id = 138&ai = a.

Kieffaber, Marilyn. "Have You Met Chris Raschka?" *Messenger*,
    July/August 2006.

Raschka, Chris. Interview with the author, July 2, 2007.

**31. Brian Sell**

"Hall Puts on Stunning Display, Wins Olympic Trials in Men's
    Marathon." *USA Track and Field*. http://www.usatf.org/news/
    view.aspx?DUID = USATF_2007_11_03_09_59_41.

Hartsock, John. "Running Down a Dream." *Altoona Mirror*,
    July 15, 2007.

Sell, Brian. Personal interview with the author, May 22, 2007.

Spring, Ryan. "Sell Earns an Olympic Berth with Third Place
    Finish." *Bedford* (Pa.) *Gazette*, November 5, 2007.

**32. Sam Hornish, Jr.**

"A Passion for Victory." The Defiance Publishing Co., 2006.

Slacian, Joseph. "There's More to Life Than Racing." Brethren.org.
    *Newsline*, 2/14/07 (reprint from *Wabash (Ind.) Plain Dealer*,
    2/11/07). http://www.brethren.org/genbd/newsline/
    2007/feb1407.htm#6.

Wiltschek, Walt. "Living a Dream." *Messenger*, November 2007.

**Frank Ramirez** has written numerous books, among them *The Meanest Man in Patrick County and Other Unlikely Brethren Heroes.* He is pastor of the Everett Church of the Brethren in Pennsylvania.

**Kermon Thomasson** served twenty years as editor of the Church of the Brethren magazine, *Messenger*, following thirteen years teaching at Waka Teachers' College in Nigeria. He lives in Henry County, Virginia.